OUR THREATENED OCEANS

The Oceans are the basis of all life. They regulate our climate, they feed us, and a visit to their shores lifts our spirits. This volume explains the fascinating facts about how the oceans work and affect all of us. It shows how we are changing our oceans through global warming, over-fishing and pollution – and what we can do to restore their health.

Stefan Rahmstorf is Professor of Physics of the Oceans at the University of Potsdam in Germany and Honorary Fellow of Bangor University in Wales. He is a member of the Advisory Council on Global Change of the German government and a lead author of the 4th IPCC Report. He has published over 50 scientific papers on the oceans and climate.

Katherine Richardson is a Professor in Biological Oceanography and a Vice Dean at the University of Copenhagen. She is active in international fora relating to global change. She has been a member of the steering committee for the International Geosphere Biosphere Program (IGBP) and an author on IGBP synthesis book "Global Change and the Earth System: A Planet under Pressure" (Springer 2004). She is currently Chairman of the Climate Commission established by the Danish Government.

Our addresses on the Internet:
www.the-sustainability-project.com
www.forum-fuer-verantwortung.de
[English version available]

OUR THREATENED OCEANS

STEFAN RAHMSTORF/KATHERINE RICHARDSON

Translated by Baker & Harrison

Klaus Wiegandt, General Editor

HAUS PUBLISHING

First published in Great Britain in 2009 by
Haus Publishing Ltd
70 Cadogan Place
London SW1X 9AH
www.hauspublishing.com

Originally published as: *Wie Bedroht Sind die Ozeane? Biologische und physikalische Aspekte*, by Stefan Rahmstorf/Katherine Richardson. Ed. by Klaus Wiegandt
© 2007 Fischer Taschenbuch Verlag in der S. Fischer Verlag GmbH, Frankfurt am Main

English translation copyright © Baker & Harrison 2008

A CIP catalogue record for this book
is available from the British Library

ISBN 978-1-906598-06-8

Typeset in Sabon by MacGuru Ltd
Printed in Dubai by Oriental Press

Mixed Sources
Product group from well-managed
forests and other controlled sources
www.fsc.org Cert no. CU-COC-809367
© 1996 Forest Stewardship Council

FSC

Haus Publishing believes in the importance of a sustainable future for our planet. This book is printed on paper produced in accordance with the standards of sustainability set out and monitored by the FSC. The printer holds chain of custody.

Contents

Editor's Foreword

Sustainability Project

Sales of the German-language edition of this series have exceeded all expectations. The positive media response has been encouraging, too. Both of these positive responses demonstrate that the series addresses the right topics in a language that is easily understood by the general reader. The combination of thematic breadth and scientifically astute, yet generally accessible writing, is particularly important as I believe it to be a vital prerequisite for smoothing the way to a sustainable society by turning knowledge into action. After all, I am not a scientist myself; my background is in business.

A few months ago, shortly after the first volumes had been published, we received suggestions from neighboring countries in Europe recommending that an English-language edition would reach a far larger readership. Books dealing with global challenges, they said, require global action brought about by informed debate amongst as large an audience as possible. When delegates from India, China, and Pakistan voiced similar concerns at an international conference my mind was made up. Dedicated individuals such as Lester R. Brown and Jonathan Porritt deserve credit for bringing the concept of sustainability to the attention of the general public, I am convinced that this series can give the discourse about sustainability something new.

Two years have passed since I wrote the foreword to the initial German edition. During this time, unsustainable developments on our planet have come to our attention in ever more dramatic ways. The price of oil has nearly tripled; the value of industrial metals has risen exponentially and, quite unexpectedly, the costs of staple foods such as corn, rice, and wheat have reached all-time highs. Around the globe, people are increasingly concerned that the pressure caused by these drastic price increases will lead to serious destabilization in China, India, Indonesia, Vietnam, and Malaysia, the world's key developing regions.

The frequency and intensity of natural disasters brought on by global warming has continued to increase. Many regions of our Earth are experiencing prolonged droughts, with subsequent shortages of drinking water and the destruction of entire harvests. In other parts of the world, typhoons and hurricanes are causing massive flooding and inflicting immeasurable suffering.

The turbulence in the world's financial markets, triggered by the US sub-prime mortgage crisis, has only added to these woes. It has affected every country and made clear just how unscrupulous and sometimes irresponsible speculation has become in today's financial world. The expectation of exorbitant short-term rates of return on capital investments led to complex and obscure financial engineering. Coupled with a reckless willingness to take risks everyone involved seemingly lost track of the situation. How else can blue chip companies incur multi-billion dollar losses? If central banks had not come to the rescue with dramatic steps to back up their currencies, the world's economy would have collapsed. It was only in these circumstances that the use of public monies could be justified. It is therefore imperative to prevent a repeat of speculation with short-term capital on such a gigantic scale.

Taken together, these developments have at least significantly improved the readiness for a debate on sustainability. Many more are now aware that our wasteful use of natural resources and energy have serious consequences, and not only for future generations.

Two years ago, who would have dared to hope that WalMart, the world's largest retailer, would initiate a dialog about sustainability with its customers and promise to put the results into practice? Who would have considered it possible that CNN would start a series "Going Green"? Every day, more and more businesses worldwide announce that they are putting the topic of sustainability at the core of their strategic considerations. Let us use this momentum to try and make sure that these positive developments are not a flash in the pan, but a solid part of our necessary discourse within civic society.

However, we cannot achieve sustainable development through a multitude of individual adjustments. We are facing the challenge of critical fundamental questioning of our lifestyle and consumption and patterns of production. We must grapple with the complexity of the entire earth system in a forward-looking and precautionary manner, and not focus solely on topics such as energy and climate change.

The authors of these twelve books examine the consequences of our destructive interference in the Earth ecosystem from different perspectives. They point out that we still have plenty of opportunities to shape a sustainable future. If we want to achieve this, however, it is imperative that we use the information we have as a basis for systematic action, guided by the principles of sustainable development. If the step from knowledge to action is not only to be taken, but also to succeed, we need to offer comprehensive education to all, with the foundation in early childhood. The central issues of the future must be anchored firmly in school curricula, and no university student should be permitted to graduate without having completed a general course on sustainable development. Everyday opportunities for action must be made clear to us all – young and old. Only then can we begin to think critically about our lifestyles and make positive changes in the direction of sustainability. We need to show the business community the way to sustainable development via a responsible attitude to consumption, and become active within our sphere of influence as opinion leaders.

For this reason, my foundation *Forum für Verantwortung*, the ASKO EUROPA-FOUNDATION, and the European Academy Otzenhausen have joined forces to produce educational materials on the future of the Earth to accompany the twelve books developed at the renowned Wuppertal Institute for Climate, Environment and Energy. We are setting up an extensive program of seminars, and the initial results are very promising. The success of our initiative "Encouraging Sustainability," which has now been awarded the status of an official project of the UN Decade "Education for Sustainable Development," confirms the public's great interest in, and demand for, well-founded information.

I would like to thank the authors for their additional effort to update all their information and put the contents of their original volumes in a more global context. My special thanks goes to the translators, who submitted themselves to a strict timetable, and to Annette Maas for coordinating the Sustainability Project. I am grateful for the expert editorial advice of Amy Irvine and the Haus Publishing editorial team for not losing track of the "3600-page-work."

Taking Action — Out of Insight and Responsibility

"We were on our way to becoming gods, supreme beings who could create a second world, using the natural world only as building blocks for our new creation."

This warning by the psychoanalyst and social philosopher Erich Fromm is to be found in *To Have or to Be?* (1976). It aptly expresses the dilemma in which we find ourselves as a result of our scientific-technical orientation.

The original intention of submitting to nature in order to make use of it ("knowledge is power") evolved into subjugating nature in order to exploit it. We have left the earlier successful path with its many advances and are now on the wrong track, a path of danger with incalculable risks. The greatest danger stems from the unshakable faith of the overwhelming majority of politicians and business leaders in unlimited economic growth which, together with limitless technological innovation, is supposed to provide solutions to all the challenges of the present and the future.

For decades now, scientists have been warning of this collision course with nature. As early as 1983, the United Nations founded the World Commission on Environment and Development which published the Brundtland Report in 1987. Under the title *Our Common Future*, it presented a concept that could save mankind from catastrophe and help to find the way back to a responsible way of life, the concept of long-term environmentally sustainable use of resources. "Sustainability," as used in the Brundtland Report, means "development that meets the needs of the present without compromising the ability of future generations to meet their own needs."

Despite many efforts, this guiding principle for ecologically, economically, and socially sustainable action has unfortunately

not yet become the reality it can, indeed must, become. I believe
the reason for this is that civil societies have not yet been sufficiently informed and mobilized.

Forum für Verantwortung

Against this background, and in the light of ever more warnings
and scientific results, I decided to take on a societal responsibility with my foundation. I would like to contribute to the
expansion of public discourse about sustainable development
which is absolutely essential. It is my desire to provide a large
number of people with facts and contextual knowledge on the
subject of sustainability, and to show alternative options for
future action.

After all, the principle of "sustainable development" alone is
insufficient to change current patterns of living and economic
practices. It does provide some orientation, but it has to be nego-
tiated in concrete terms within society and then implemented
in patterns of behavior. A democratic society seriously seeking
to reorient itself towards future viability must rely on critical,
creative individuals capable of both discussion and action. For
this reason, life-long learning, from childhood to old age, is a
necessary precondition for realizing sustainable development.
The practical implementation of the ecological, economic,
and social goals of a sustainability strategy in economic policy
requires people able to reflect, innovate and recognize potentials
for structural change and learn to use them in the best interests
of society.

It is not enough for individuals to be merely "concerned."
On the contrary, it is necessary to understand the scientific
background and interconnections in order to have access to

them and be able to develop them in discussions that lead in the right direction. Only in this way can the ability to make appropriate judgments emerge, and this is a prerequisite for responsible action.

The essential condition for this is presentation of both the facts and the theories within whose framework possible courses of action are visible in a manner that is both appropriate to the subject matter and comprehensible. Then, people will be able to use them to guide their personal behavior.

In order to move towards this goal, I asked renowned scientists to present in a generally understandable way the state of research and the possible options on twelve important topics in the area of sustainable development in the series "*Forum für Verantwortung*." All those involved in this project are in agreement that there is no alternative to a united path of all societies towards sustainability:

— *Our Planet: How Much More Can Earth Take?* (Jill Jäger)
— *Energy: The World's Race for Resources in the 21st Century* (Hermann-Joseph Wagner)
— *Our Threatened Oceans* (Stefan Rahmstorf and Katherine Richardson)
— *Water Resources: Efficient, Sustainable and Equitable Use* (Wolfram Mauser)
— *The Earth: Natural Resources and Human Intervention* (Friedrich Schmidt-Bleek)
— *Overcrowded World? Global Population and International Migration* (Rainer Münz and Albert F. Reiterer)
— *Feeding the Planet: Environmental Protection through Sustainable Agriculture* (Klaus Hahlbrock)
— *Costing the Earth? Perspectives on Sustainable Development* (Bernd Meyer)

- *The New Plagues: Pandemics and Poverty in a Globalized World* (Stefan Kaufmann)
- *Climate Change: The Point of No Return* (Mojib Latif)
- *The Demise of Diversity: Loss and Extinction* (Josef H Reichholf)
- *Building a New World Order: Sustainable Policies for the Future* (Harald Müller)

The public debate

What gives me the courage to carry out this project and the optimism that I will reach civil societies in this way, and possibly provide an impetus for change?

For one thing, I have observed that, because of the number and severity of natural disasters in recent years, people have become more sensitive concerning questions of how we treat the Earth. For another, there are scarcely any books on the market that cover in language comprehensible to civil society the broad spectrum of comprehensive sustainable development in an integrated manner.

When I began to structure my ideas and the prerequisites for a public discourse on sustainability in 2004, I could not foresee that by the time the first books of the series were published, the general public would have come to perceive at least climate change and energy as topics of great concern. I believe this occurred especially as a result of the following events:

First, the United States witnessed the devastation of New Orleans in August 2005 by Hurricane Katrina, and the anarchy following in the wake of this disaster.

Second, in 2006, Al Gore began his information campaign on climate change and wastage of energy, culminating in his film *An*

Inconvenient Truth, which has made an impression on a wide audience of all age groups around the world.

Third, the 700-page Stern Report, commissioned by the British government, published in 2007 by the former Chief Economist of the World Bank Nicholas Stern in collaboration with other economists, was a wake-up call for politicians and business leaders alike. This report makes clear how extensive the damage to the global economy will be if we continue with "business as usual" and do not take vigorous steps to halt climate change. At the same time, the report demonstrates that we could finance countermeasures for just one-tenth of the cost of the probable damage, and could limit average global warming to 2° C – if we only took action.

Fourth, the most recent IPCC report, published in early 2007, was met by especially intense media interest, and therefore also received considerable public attention. It laid bare as never before how serious the situation is, and called for drastic action against climate change.

Last, but not least, the exceptional commitment of a number of billionaires such as Bill Gates, Warren Buffett, George Soros, and Richard Branson as well as Bill Clinton's work to "save the world" is impressing people around the globe and deserves mention here.

An important task for the authors of our twelve-volume series was to provide appropriate steps towards sustainable development in their particular subject area. In this context, we must always be aware that successful transition to this type of economic, ecological, and social development on our planet cannot succeed immediately, but will require many decades. Today, there are still no sure formulae for the most successful long-term path. A large number of scientists and even more innovative entrepreneurs and managers will have to use their creativity and dynamism to solve the great challenges. Nonetheless, even today, we can discern the first clear goals we must reach in order to avert a looming catastrophe. And billions of consumers around the world can use their daily purchasing decisions to help both ease and significantly accelerate the economy's transition to sustainable development – provided the political framework is there. In addition, from a global perspective, billions of citizens have the opportunity to mark out the political "guide rails" in a democratic way via their parliaments.

The most important insight currently shared by the scientific, political, and economic communities is that our resource-intensive Western model of prosperity (enjoyed today by one billion people) cannot be extended to another five billion or, by 2050, at least eight billion people. That would go far beyond the biophysical capacity of the planet. This realization is not in dispute. At issue, however, are the consequences we need to draw from it.

If we want to avoid serious conflicts between nations, the industrialized countries must reduce their consumption of resources by more than the developing and threshold countries increase theirs. In the future, all countries must achieve the same level of consumption. Only then will we be able to create the necessary ecological room for maneuver in order to ensure an appropriate level of prosperity for developing and threshold countries.

To avoid a dramatic loss of prosperity in the West during this long-term process of adaptation, the transition from high to low resource use, that is, to an ecological market economy, must be set in motion quickly.

On the other hand, the threshold and developing countries must commit themselves to getting their population growth under control within the foreseeable future. The twenty-year Programme of Action adopted by the United Nations International Conference on Population and Development in Cairo in 1994 must be implemented with stronger support from the industrialized nations.

If humankind does not succeed in drastically improving resource and energy efficiency and reducing population growth in a sustainable manner – we should remind ourselves of the United Nations forecast that population growth will come to a halt only at the end of this century, with a world population of eleven to twelve billion – then we run the real risk of developing eco-dictatorships. In the words of Ernst Ulrich von Weizsäcker: "States will be sorely tempted to ration limited resources, to micromanage economic activity, and in the interest of the environment to specify from above what citizens may or may not do. 'Quality-of-life' experts might define in an authoritarian way what kind of needs people are permitted to satisfy." (*Earth Politics*, 1989, in English translation: 1994).

It is time

It is time for us to take stock in a fundamental and critical way. We, the public, must decide what kind of future we want. Progress and quality of life is not dependent on year-by-year growth in per capita income alone, nor do we need inexorably growing amounts of goods to satisfy our needs. The short-term goals of our economy, such as maximizing profits and accumulating capital, are major obstacles to sustainable development. We should go back to a more decentralized economy and reduce world trade and the waste of energy associated with it in a targeted fashion. If resources and energy were to cost their "true" prices, the global process of rationalization and labor displacement will be reversed, because cost pressure will be shifted to the areas of materials and energy.

The path to sustainability requires enormous technological innovations. But not everything that is technologically possible has to be put into practice. We should not strive to place all areas of our lives under the dictates of the economic system. Making justice and fairness a reality for everyone is not only a moral and ethical imperative, but is also the most important means of securing world peace in the long term. For this reason, it is essential to place the political relationship between states and peoples on a new basis, a basis with which everyone can identify, not only the most powerful. Without common principles of global governance, sustainability cannot become a reality in any of the fields discussed in this series.

And finally, we must ask whether we humans have the right to reproduce to such an extent that we may reach a population of eleven to twelve billion by the end of this century, laying claim to every square centimeter of our Earth and restricting and destroying the habitats and way of life of all other species to an ever greater degree.

Our future is not predetermined. We ourselves shape it by our actions. We can continue as before, but if we do so, we will put ourselves in the biophysical straitjacket of nature, with possibly disastrous political implications, by the middle of this century. But we also have the opportunity to create a fairer and more viable future for ourselves and for future generations. This requires the commitment of everyone on our planet.

Klaus Wiegandt

Summer 2008

1 Oceans and their Role in the Global Climate

Looking at the Earth from space, we immediately recognize it as a water planet. It moves through space like a blue pearl, unique among the planets in our solar system. Of all the known planets, the Earth is the only one to have oceans – and they cover 71% of its surface. It has, therefore, been suggested that "Ocean" would be a much more apt name for our planet than "Earth."

The dominant theory on the origin of this water holds that steam continually rose from the interior of the hot, young Earth. Once the surface had cooled below boiling point, incessant rains began to fall, and all this water accumulated in low-lying regions. This abundance of water has many profound implications – most importantly, it is the reason for the existence of life on Earth.

Geographical background

Let us start this book by familiarizing ourselves with some key facts about the world's oceans (see also Figure I in the color section): with a surface area of around 361 million km² and an average depth of 3800 meters, the oceans amount to a total volume of 1370 million km³. Over 97% of the water on our planet is in the oceans, 2% is locked up in ice sheets (mainly in Greenland and Antarctica), 0.02% in the world's lakes, rivers and reservoirs, and 0.001% is in the atmosphere at any given time.

About half of the ocean floor consists of the vast, relatively flat abyssal plains which are typically found at a depth of between 3000 and 5000 meters below the surface. These plains are covered in sediment which is made up of material that sinks down from the water column above – this material is, as a rule, the product of biological activity. The deep ocean floor is thus like a sort of planetary garbage dump where, under the influence of gravity, most of the Earth's mobile particles eventually end up. The abyssal plains are bounded by the continental slopes, where the sea floor rises up to shallow shelf seas, such as the North Sea, which surround most of the continents. These shelf seas are typically 100–200 meters deep.

The deep ocean also contains the huge mountain ranges of the mid-oceanic ridges, as well as large underwater volcanoes which rise from the abyss. Some of these breach the surface and form well known features such as the Hawaiian Islands. There are also deep trenches such as the Marianas Trench in the North Pacific, which extends to a maximum depth of 10,923 meters.

These basic features of ocean topography can be explained by plate tectonics: the movement of the oceanic and continental plates of the Earth's crust. As continental plates consist of lighter material than oceanic plates, they sink less into the soft material below and, consequently, lie higher than oceanic plates. Shallow shelf seas exist wherever the ocean water reaches over the edges of the continental plates; many of these shelf seas did not exist at the height of the last ice age, when sea levels were 120 meters lower due to the far greater volumes of water bound up in continental ice sheets. The steep continental slopes form the edges of the continental plates, while the abyssal plains are the surfaces of the oceanic plates. As everything floats on the Earth's soft mantle, the relative heights of the continental and oceanic plates are defined by their different densities and the weight of water bearing down on the ocean floor. As a result, the ocean water just reaches the level of the continental plates.

At mid-oceanic ridges, new ocean floor is formed as oceanic plates move apart allowing new material to rise from the Earth's interior. Deep trenches form in regions where a part of an oceanic plate is pushed down underneath a continental plate, for example off the coast of Japan.

Of special interest are nearly enclosed marginal seas like the Mediterranean Sea, the North Sea, the Baltic Sea, and the Sea of Japan, which historically were favorable for shipping and trade and have always supported large coastal populations. Today, the limited exchange of water with the open seas means that these regions now face a number of problems associated with waste accumulation.

The ocean water

For oceanographers, oceans are not just filled with water — instead, they see a range of distinct water masses, each with its own special "flavor" and vintage, just like a fine wine. These water masses have names and abbreviations like North Atlantic Deep Water (NADW), Sargasso Sea Water, Antarctic Bottom Water (AABW), or North Pacific Intermediate Water. There are even names for water masses that are thought to have existed tens of thousands of years ago, like the Glacial North Atlantic Intermediate Water (GNAIW), a water mass that filled the bulk of the upper part of the northern Atlantic during the last ice age.

The two most important properties that define different water masses are their temperature and salinity, and we will look at these in more detail below. However, other characteristics such as the oxygen and nutrient content, acidity and calcium carbonate saturation are also very important to marine life. Oceanographers also analyze the age of a water mass – by that they mean the time that has elapsed since that particular water sank below the ocean surface and was last in contact with the atmosphere. This is important, as the water composition changes when in it comes into contact with air: the oxygen content increases, and the fraction of unstable carbon isotopes is reset to that of the atmosphere, where the radioactive carbon isotope ^{14}C is continually produced by the effects of cosmic rays. When the water leaves the surface and sinks down to the deep, its ^{14}C concentration slowly declines due to the radioactive decay of the isotope, and this fact can be used to measure the age of the water. At an age of around 2000 years, the oldest water is found deep down in the northern Pacific. One can, thus, estimate a "turnover time" of the ocean: waters sink down at an average rate of about 0.04 km^3 per second, so that the total ocean volume given above is replenished about once every thousand years.

Ocean temperatures

It is obvious that the temperatures of the oceans are primarily governed by the unequal distribution of sunshine on our planet. While the surface waters in tropical latitudes are warm at around 30 °C, in polar latitudes they are not far from freezing point (which is close to -2 °C for salt water). The warmest open ocean water is found at the surface in the western tropical Pacific, the so-called "warm pool." Its annual mean temperature is up to 30 °C. Even warmer water can be found in some shallow coastal seas during the summer months.

Temperature (°C)

▇ 6–8	▇ 12 –14
▇ –2–0	▇ 2–4	▇ 8–10	▇ 14 –16
▇ 0–2	▇ 4–6	▇ 10 –12	▇ 16 –18

▢ 18–20   ▢ 24–26   ▢ 30–32
▢ 20–22   ▢ 26–28   ▢ > 32
▢ 22–24   ▢ 28–30

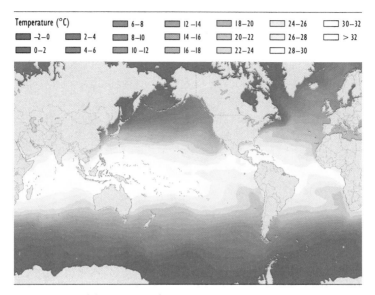

Figure 1.1 Map of the ocean surface temperatures (°C) in May 2006
based on satellite measurements

However, the sun only penetrates the surface of the world's oceans, not their vast, dark depths. Most ocean water is, in fact, very cold: 80% of the ocean's volume is below 5°C. The reason is simple: in polar latitudes, water sinks from the surface and this cold water fills the deep seas worldwide (we will discuss this later in the section about ocean currents). In contrast, the warm waters of the tropics and subtropics are light and form only a relatively thin surface layer, of a few hundred meters, which floats on top of the cold deep. This was first noticed in 1751 by Henry Ellis, the captain of an English slave trading ship, who collected deep sea water in the subtropical Atlantic with the help of a long rope and a "bucket sea gage" provided to him by a

British clergyman, the Reverend Stephen Hales. Ellis found that the water he brought up from about a mile deep was cold: the temperature measured on deck was only 12°C. A letter written by Ellis to Hales suggests he had no inkling of the far-reaching significance of his discovery. He wrote: "This experiment, which seem'd at first but mere food for curiosity, became in the interim very useful to us. By its means we supplied our cold bath, and cooled our wines or water at pleasure; which is vastly agreeable to us in this burning climate."

Why is sea water salty?

The water cycle continually moves particles from the land to the ocean. Rain falls on rock or other surfaces and dissolves minerals. The world's rivers, therefore, carry an estimated 4 billion tons of salts every year to the ocean. The salts are left behind when the water evaporates again from the surface. They then accumulate in the ocean, where they reach a much higher concentration than in river water – even reaching the point where just as much salt falls out as is continuously added, resulting in an equilibrium. Most of the substances which fall out of the water end up as sediment at the ocean floor, eventually being swept into the Earth's crust, when that particular region of sea floor is pushed under a continental plate. Just like the world's oceans, all other water bodies with no outflow also act as traps for dissolved particles and are therefore salty, e.g. the Great Salt Lake in Utah or the Caspian Sea.

Different dissolved substances are removed from ocean water in different ways. Some simply exceed the saturation level, so that no more can be dissolved and any excess will fall out. Others undergo chemical reactions. Some, like silicon and calcium, are eagerly used by organisms for building shells, tiny or large. For these substances, the raining of shells down into the sediments provides the main mechanism for their removal from the water column (in many places sediments are made up predominantly of these shells).

Chloride and sodium (the components of ordinary table salt) make up 85% of the dissolved substances in ocean water. The reason for their abundance is that their solubility in water is high and they are not removed by biological mechanisms. The average salt content of the ocean is 35 grams per kilogram of sea water. That is 3.5%, but, traditionally, oceanographers report the salt content of ocean water as per mille, i.e. they say 35‰. Based on the total ocean volume given above, we conclude there must be about 5×10^{16} tons of salt in the ocean. With the input of 4×10^9 tons per year, we obtain an average dwelling time of about 10^7 years, or ten million years. This is orders of magnitude longer than the timescale for the mixing of ocean waters by currents and turbulence and we can, therefore, expect the main salts to be extremely well-mixed throughout the global ocean. Indeed, the composition of sea salt is almost exactly the same everywhere – that was one of many findings of the famous *Challenger* expedition in the late 19th century, the first global oceanographic expedition.

This fact makes life much simpler for oceanographers – instead of measuring a host of different salts, they only need to report the total salt concentration, which they call salinity. To measure salinity they can use the electrical conductivity of the water. The salinity is of great dynamical importance as, together with temperature and pressure (which increases with depth), it determines the density of sea water and, therefore, affects both the pressure distribution in the sea and ocean currents.

Variations in salinity in the ocean are governed by the sources and sinks of freshwater and not by the sources and sinks of salts, as the former are orders of magnitude larger than the latter. Every year, over 4×10^{14} cubic meters of water evaporate from the ocean (a net loss of about one meter each year), so its total water amount is replaced about every 3000 years – which is nothing in comparison with the ten million years it takes for the salt to be replaced. We therefore find high salinity wherever evaporation exceeds precipitation, namely in the warm and dry subtropics, and low salinity in the high latitudes or, on a smaller scale, near river mouths. Near the equator, the extensive cloud cover and high rainfall of the inter-tropical convergence zone (the famous tropical rainfall belts) lead to relatively low salinities.

In most of the world's oceans away from the coasts, salinity is between 33 and 38‰. Some semi-enclosed seas can, of course, have very different values. The Baltic Sea, where rainfall and river inflow greatly exceed evaporation, exhibits salinities ranging from about 5‰ at the Finnish end to 15‰ at the Skagerrak, its shallow connection with the North Sea and the global ocean. At the other extreme, the Red Sea and Persian Gulf have salinities near 40‰ as the evaporation rates are so high here. The Mediterranean Sea is also a basin which loses more freshwater than is added (about one meter each year) and a vigorous two-way flow through the Straits of Gibraltar is required to balance its water and salinity budgets: a flow which brings relatively fresh water into the Mediterranean at the surface and a saline outflow below it.

The ocean's currents

The oceans are perpetually in motion. Three types of force cause this movement.

The first of these are the tidal forces, the gravitational pull of the Moon and Sun which cause the familiar oscillations of the tides. Essentially, tides are the result of the Moon pulling a "bulge" of ocean water upwards. As a result of this, the water level is higher where the Moon is overhead, while the Earth rotates beneath it. What is not quite so obvious is why, in most places in the world, high tide occurs twice daily, not just once. This is because of a second bulge of water on the opposite side of Earth, caused by centrifugal force. As the Earth moves in "free fall" in the Moon's gravity field, centrifugal force and gravity are exactly balanced at the center of the Earth. On the surface of the side facing the Moon, the Moon's gravity is stronger, pulling the water surface upward. On the far side of Earth, its gravity is weaker, causing the water to sag away from the Moon, which is again upward as seen from Earth. This double bulge causes the twice-daily tidal cycle.

The superposition of a similar, but weaker, effect of the Sun's gravity causes the so-called spring and neap tide cycle. Spring tides (not to be confused with storm surges) occur every fortnight, when the Moon and the Sun are aligned and their gravitational effects on the Earth's oceans add up, as the moon takes 29 days to orbit Earth.

This simple picture would offer a correct description for the "equilibrium tides" if our planet was completely covered in water. However, matters are complicated by coastlines and by the fact that so much water cannot be moved fast enough to keep up with the Moon moving along overhead – as we know from air travel, keeping up with the Earth's rotation requires travel at more than the speed of sound. The deflection of water movements by the Earth's rotation (see below) also plays a role in the way tides move. In reality, then, the tidal bulges rotate around the large ocean basins and interact with the coasts. In some places, the shape of the coastline leads to a resonance which results in a particularly large tidal range. Such places are good locations for tidal energy generation. The Bay of Fundy in eastern Canada is famed for having the largest tidal range in the world, with over 15 meters in the vertical at the head of the bay.

The second force which causes water to move is the wind. Surface waves and currents are caused as a result of the friction between the winds and the water. While the tidal currents completely reverse direction four times a day and, therefore, simply "slosh water back and forth," other currents can transport water over long distances. For most people, the way these large-scale currents move is counter-intuitive. This is because our Earth is a rotating sphere, and currents are deflected by the Coriolis force (which, strictly speaking, is not a force at all, but merely an illusion experienced by an observer in a rotating reference system). For example, a steady wind from the east will, overall, move water towards the north in the northern hemisphere (more generally, at a 90° angle to the right of the wind) and towards the south in the southern hemisphere (90° to the left). This is why the easterly trade winds, which blow in tropical latitudes, push water away from the equator in both hemispheres. This water has to be replaced by water rising from below near the equator. This "equatorial upwelling" of water is an important oceanographic phenomenon, not least because it provides nutrients to surface waters in the equatorial zone.

Major features of the wind-driven ocean circulation are the great subtropical gyres, which exist in each ocean basin between about 15 and 50 degrees of latitude. They are like giant water wheels spinning in the horizontal in the upper few hundred meters of ocean. On their western sides, the flow of these gyres is in narrow and rapid boundary currents flowing polewards: the Gulf Stream in the North Atlantic, the Kuroshio in the North Pacific, the Brazil Current in the South Atlantic or the East

Australia Current in the South Pacific. The return flow towards the equator, on the other hand, is wider and more sluggish, spread out over almost the entire width of the relevant ocean basin. It was an important breakthrough in oceanography when, in the 1940s, Henry Stommel found the theoretical explanation for this "westward intensification:" the cause is the conservation law for angular momentum on the rotating Earth.

In the center of each subtropical gyre, there is a huge and nearly uniform water mass, where surface waters converge and slowly sink several hundreds of meters. In the North Atlantic, this water mass is the Sargasso Sea, with its legendary accumulation of thick seaweed mats that Alexander von Humboldt described so vividly in his "Views of Nature" (1807). According to information gleaned from studies of log books kept since Columbus' sightings of these seaweed mats, Humboldt was particularly fascinated by the fact that, for several centuries, the sea grass could be found in the same place: "Such evidences of the persistence of great natural phenomena doubly arrest the attention of the natural philosopher when they occur in the ever-moving oceanic element" (*On Steppes and Deserts*, annotation 7).

This brings us to describe the third of the major driving forces of ocean currents, in addition to tidal forces and winds: "thermohaline forcing." By this, we mean the exchange of heat and freshwater at the ocean surface which makes the water warmer or colder, saltier or fresher. The syllable "thermo" stands for temperature change, and "haline" stands for salinity change (from the Greek word for salt). As was already explained above, temperature and salinity changes affect the density of the water, and density differences cause pressure differences in the fluid. Pressure differences, of course, will drive currents.

The most important feature of thermohaline forcing is that it determines where water can sink from the surface to the deep ocean: this happens where the density of surface water is greatest. Surface densities close to 1028 kg/m³ are only reached in three regions of the world's oceans: in the northern Atlantic (specifically in the Labrador Sea and the Greenland-Norwegian Sea), around Antarctica (in the Ross and Weddell Seas), and in the Mediterranean Sea. In the first two regions, the high density is mainly due to the cold temperatures, while in the Mediterranean it is the result of high salinity. The influence of the Mediterranean on the global ocean is limited because it is only connected to the Atlantic via the shallow Straits of Gibraltar. However, the processes occurring in the two polar regions have a profound effect on the entire global ocean system.

It is in these polar regions that water sinks, in a process called "deep water formation" and then spreads around the world at depth. The deep and bottom waters of the world ocean originate from this deep water formation. Return flows near the surface move water towards these "ocean plugholes," where they replace what has sunk. This results in a gigantic overturning motion of the world's oceans (Plate 3 in the color section) which moves at a rate of around 30 Sv. ("Sv" stands for "Sverdrup," an historic oceanographic unit for flow named after the Swedish oceanographer Harald Ulrik Sverdrup. 1 Sv = 1 cubic meters per second.)

Once the deep ocean is filled with this high-density water, water from other regions with a lower density is, obviously, prevented from sinking – these lower density water masses must float on top of the denser water. Alert readers may note a paradox here: once the ocean has been filled with water of the highest

Figure 1.2 The main surface currents of the world's oceans. The great subtropical gyres, which are found in all the large ocean basins, are shown in light blue

The oceans and global climate

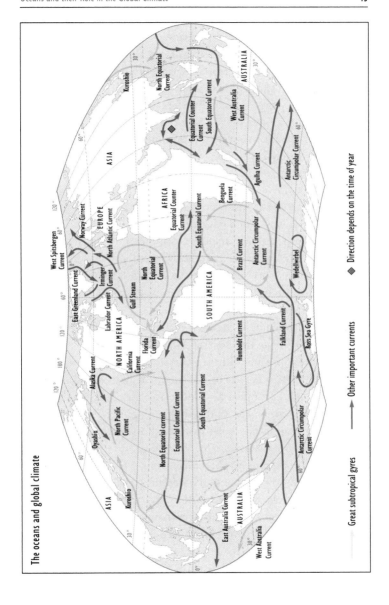

Great subtropical gyres

⟶ Other important currents

◆ Direction depends on the time of year

density, why would *any* water continue to sink? And why would the grand overturning of the oceans not simply grind to a halt? The main reason is that turbulence in the ocean slowly mixes heat down from the warm surface layers into the depths, thus reducing the density of deeper waters over time. This continual loss of density allows for an ongoing replacement of the deep waters with "young" source waters from polar latitudes.

In the 19th century, there was intense debate among scholars as to what it is that drives the major ocean currents such as the Gulf Stream: wind forcing or thermohaline forcing? Were these currents wind-driven currents, or were they "convection currents", as it was called back then?

In some respects, this dispute is still not fully resolved today. We now know that many currents, including the Gulf Stream, are a mixture of both driving forces such that wind driving and thermohaline forcing both play a significant role but quantifying how much each contributes is difficult.

The Gulf Stream is the western boundary current of the subtropical gyre in the North Atlantic – as such, we introduced it above as a wind-driven current. However, a northward surface flow, which is part of the thermohaline overturning just discussed, is superimposed – and this also contributes to the Gulf Stream flow. In the mid-latitude Atlantic, the magnitude of this overturning has been estimated at 15–20 Sv. The total Gulf Stream flow is about 70 Sv (if local counter flows are taken into account). We might, therefore, choose to say that about a quarter of the flow of the Gulf Stream is thermohaline-driven and three quarters wind-driven. However, this is only a rough estimate, as wind-driven and thermohaline currents in the ocean interact in non-linear ways and there is no method to strictly differentiate them.

The strongest ocean current on Earth circles the Antarctic

continent: the Antarctic Circumpolar Current. With a flow of 120 to 140 Sv, this is over a thousand times the flow of the Amazon River. Its flow reaches from the surface right down to the bottom of the ocean. Both the westerly winds and thermohaline forcing (cooling around Antarctica) contribute to this massive flow but the main reason for its might is the fact that it is not impeded by continents. On a rotating sphere, winds and ocean currents have a natural tendency to flow in bands aligned with the latitudes, like the westerly wind belt. However, for ocean currents, this path is blocked everywhere by continents – except between 56° and 63° south, the latitudes of Drake Passage. Here, the Antarctic Circumpolar Current can circle the globe in west-east direction unimpeded by continental barriers.

Quite unlike the simplified diagrams seen in atlases (and also in this book) may suggest, the flow of real ocean currents is not straight and steady. Most of them are highly turbulent and unsteady flows, with many meanders and eddies which are constantly changing. Satellites provide vivid images of these meanders, as do the high-resolution ocean circulation models that oceanographic research institutions run on their supercomputers. These eddies and meanders are widespread in the ocean and arise automatically in computer models because of instabilities in the underlying hydrodynamic flow equations.

Turbulence in the ocean is very important as it mixes components such as heat, salt and nutrients – and, through this mixing, turbulence has a profound effect on ocean water density and large-scale currents, on the dispersal of pollutants, and on biological productivity. One of the grand challenges of physical oceanography today is to better understand and model the properties of this turbulence – that is, its regional distribution and how it changes over time.

Waves

Waves are another fascinating phenomenon of ocean dynamics. Surfers travel the world in search of the perfect breaking wave, while designers of structures like sea walls and offshore oil rigs need to carefully incorporate the massive forces that waves can unleash in their designs. On 1 November 2006, for example, the first autumn storm of the year in the North Sea caused waves of up to 20 meters high, tearing loose a Norwegian oil platform with 75 men on board. Fortunately, they were all rescued.

Most waves are caused by the action of the wind on the surface of the water. Large waves caused by storms can travel thousands of kilometers. Along their route, they are sorted by wavelength, as waves of different wavelength travel at different speeds. Far away from the storm that caused them, these waves therefore arrive as an extremely regular swell. They break when they reach shallow water, as they are slowed down from below and the crests overtake the troughs.

In extreme cases, submarine earthquakes and underwater landslides can cause very long surface waves called tsunamis (which are sometimes incorrectly referred to as "tidal waves"). They can race across entire ocean basins within hours and cause major destruction when they pile up at a coast. Their long wavelengths of 100–700 km make them very fast, and they reach speeds of up to about 700 km/h. Out in the open ocean, even large and dangerous tsunamis are only about 30 centimeters high and, in a boat out at sea, one would not notice a tsunami passing underneath. However, like wind-generated waves, tsunamis gain greatly in height when they are slowed down and squeezed together when they reach shallow coastal waters.

The tsunami of 26 December 2004 caused the death of almost 300,000 people along the coasts of the Indian Ocean. An Atlantic earthquake and tsunami destroyed the port city of Lisbon on 1 November 1755 and, in 1883, the eruption of Krakatoa caused a major tsunami to hit Indonesia. In the Pacific Ocean, a tsunami warning system has been in operation since 1946: computer models are used to predict the propagation of the tsunami waves when a potentially dangerous submarine earthquake is detected. Coastal populations are then warned by radio broadcasts, sirens and other means if a tsunami is approaching.

As well as full-scale tsunamis, there are also smaller "meteo tsunamis," which are triggered by certain fluctuations in air pressure and have been noted in the past, predominantly in the Mediterranean. They give rise to mysteriously large waves, which occur out of the blue in seaports like Ciutadella on the island of Menorca and, occasionally, result in significant damage. To the locals, these sudden waves have different names: in Menorca they are called *Rissaga*, in Malta *Milghuba* and in Sicily *Marrubio*.

Most people only think of the ocean *surface* when they hear about waves but, in fact, waves also occur in the ocean interior. Usually, these waves are completely invisible at the surface. Waves and other oscillations typically develop when something is displaced from an equilibrium position and a "return force" pulls it back – i.e. gravity when some water is displaced upwards from a flat water surface. Such a return force also arises when water is displaced vertically *inside* the ocean. This happens because the ocean is stratified: as discussed above, relatively light waters float on top of heavier waters. A familiar example is oil floating on top of vinegar in a jar of salad dressing before it is mixed – at the oil-vinegar interface, waves can be started that leave the surface completely unruffled. The interior ocean is full of such waves, which are called "internal waves." They have a very low frequency but large amplitudes, as the return force here is much weaker than that acting at the surface due to the lower density contrast. These internal waves can travel and break like surface waves and are thus an important source of turbulence inside the ocean.

The coastlines

The coast, where ocean meets land, is a special place for many people. Holidaymakers are drawn to the coasts, many of the world's largest cities, including New York, Tokyo, Shanghai and Mumbai are directly on the coast and, for many millennia, people living along coasts have earned their living from fishing and other maritime activities. Today, about 300 million people live below five meters of elevation above mean sea level, a point we will revisit in Chapter 4 when discussing sea level rise.

There is a tremendous amount of coastline on Earth. The exact length depends on the length of the ruler one uses to measure it, as the coastline has a fractal shape and becomes longer and longer the more fine undulations one includes in the measurement. However, as a rough estimate and measured with a "ruler" of a few kilometers length, the world has about one million kilometers of coastline. This sounds like quite a lot but it is worth noting that if we lined up all six billion people that currently live on this planet along the world's coasts, it would be very crowded, with six people to each meter. This perspective may help us to understand why human activities can have a major impact on the oceans.

Coastlines are not static but constantly shaped by the incessant interaction of the water with the land. Most important of all these interactions is the energetic action of waves, which shapes the coastal zone and the profile of the offshore floor of the ocean. Waves provide energy that erodes the coastline. In addition, they suspend sediment particles in the water. Incoming waves drive coastal currents which transport sand. Under some conditions, they also cause offshore rip currents that can be dangerous for inexperienced swimmers. In general, in an environment with strong winds and high-energy waves, beaches tend to consist of coarser material (coarse sand, pebbles or stones) and tend to be steep. At quieter coasts, such as those frequently found in the tropics or protected bays, beaches consist of fine sand and are often broad and gently sloping. A large tidal range favors the formation of wide beaches.

The amount of erosion on a coastline is also determined by the geological conditions, with hard rocks (like basalt) providing much more resistance to erosion than weaker material (such as sandstone). Sandstone coasts often erode and retreat rapidly, as can be seen by tiny remnant islands a few tens or hundreds of meters offshore.

Beach material from eroding headlands or river mouths is transported away by currents and waves and accumulates in sheltered places, like bays or the quieter sea floor. Wind can also blow sand inland and form dunes, that eventually become stabilized by vegetation. The shape of the beach can change over time, adjusting to changes in wind conditions or, over longer time scales, changes in sea level. Alongshore transport of sand often causes sand banks, such as Farewell Spit in New Zealand, or barrier islands like Sylt in the eastern North Sea. Oceanographers study the dynamics of such changes in large wave tanks with artificial beaches.

A special and favorite type of coastal setting is the mouths of rivers. Humans have preferred to settle in such locations since the dawn of civilization, as river mouths provide fertile plains for agriculture as well as opportunities for fishing. In addition, they also often provide sheltered harbors and the river allows for easy transport inland as well as for waste disposal.

To understand the shape of river mouths, one must realize that the sea level rose by 120 meters at the end of the last ice age, until about 5000 years ago. River mouths in flat coastal plains are thus simply rivers of the Pleistocene that have been flooded by the rising seas. At higher latitudes, where glaciers have carved steep valleys right down to the sea during the ice age (i.e., in Norway or southern New Zealand), these flooded valleys are now spectacularly beautiful fjords with sometimes almost vertical walls. At river mouths, the light and fresh river outflow meets the salty and heavier sea water, giving rise to special ecological conditions, as well as special types of circulation.

How the oceans influence climate

We have now familiarized ourselves with some of the key geographical and dynamical features of the oceans: the ocean basins, water masses, currents, waves and coastlines. But what role do the oceans play in the climate system? In a nutshell, they do five crucial things: they store heat, they transport heat around the globe, they provide water to the atmosphere, they freeze, and they store and exchange gases like carbon dioxide with the atmosphere. The oceans are, thus, an integral part of the climate system and are as important as the atmosphere. We will explain these factors in turn.

The fact that most of the Earth is covered by oceans, while the atmosphere is largely transparent to solar radiation, means that most of the sun's energy is first absorbed by the oceans. The oceans store this heat, move it around the planet through ocean currents and eventually release it back into the atmosphere. The oceans thus provide a key control for how solar energy enters and drives the climate system.

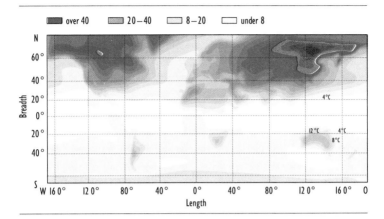

Figure 1.3 The seasonal differences in global climate

The temperature difference between the warmest and coldest months of the year (on average over many years) are shown here. The oceans moderate the seasons considerably.

The large capacity of the oceans to store heat provides a buffering effect that reduces variations in climate. A prime example here is the seasonal variation in climate: most people are aware of the fact that maritime climates experience much smaller seasonal differences than continental climates (Fig. 1.3). In the interior of North America, for example, the difference between summer and winter temperatures is 44° C and in Siberia it is even 56° C. By contrast, near coasts at the same latitudes, the seasonal range is usually less than 8 °C.

This heat storage capacity of the oceans also leads to a delay in seasonal temperature changes. The maximum of solar radiation in the northern hemisphere is reached on 20 June (the astronomical starting date of summer) but the warmest temperatures are reached in late July in continental climates, and in August in maritime climates, while sea surface temperatures peak only in September.

This seasonal heat storage does not involve the whole ocean but only a thin surface layer, the so-called "mixed layer." The reason is simple: almost all of the sun's rays are absorbed in the top few meters of ocean water (the exact depth of penetration depends on how clear the water is). Bringing this heat further down into the water column would require an input of energy, because warm water is lighter than cold water and naturally floats on top. Such an energy input is provided by the wind, which stirs the upper tens of meters of water and thus mixes the heat downward. The thickness of this mixed layer depends on the balance of how much wind energy is available for mixing and how much is required to stir heat down to a certain depth. In summer, the mixed layer is shallow (a few tens of meters) while, in winter, it can become quite deep (typically around 100–200 meters) because surface cooling makes the water heavier which helps the mixing. As discussed above, in the regions in which the highest water densities are reached in winter, the water sinks down and – over the course of millennia – fills the deep oceans of the world. The warm surface waters in the tropics and subtropics are floating as a thin layer on top of this mass of cold water.

This heat buffering effect of the oceans is not only important in terms of how it reduces the impact of the seasons but also on the longer time scales of climatic changes. Here, not only the surface mixed layer but also deeper layers become involved in storing large amounts of heat, causing a delay in the response to the climate system to perturbations at the surface. For the current rise in global temperatures (discussed in more detail in Chapter 4), it is estimated that ocean heat uptake (according to ocean temperature measurements about 0.6 Watts per square meter of the Earth's surface) accounts for between a third and half of the

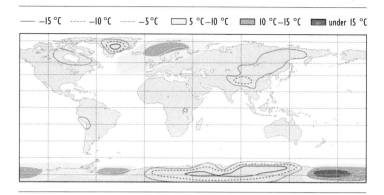

—— –15 °C   ····· –10 °C   ········ –5 °C   ☐ 5 °C–10 °C   ▨ 10 °C–15 °C   ▩ under 15 °C

Figure 1.4 The deviations of climatic temperatures from the average
value for each circle of latitude

The air temperatures over the areas of deep water formation of the world's
oceans in the North Atlantic and Antarctic Ocean are more than 10° C higher
than normal for the degree of latitude.

perturbation to the energy budget caused by humans. In other
words, if humans have caused an additional influx of heat of
1.6 Watts (the number is somewhat uncertain as this is not only
due to greenhouse gases but partly offset by the more uncertain
aerosol cooling effect) and the ocean takes up 0.6 Watts of that,
then we are only feeling the effects of the remaining 1.0 Watts
(all per square meter). Up to half of the surface warming already
caused by us is not yet felt by us but has "disappeared" into the
ocean for now, masked by the (still) cool ocean waters, until they
gradually warm up over the coming decades.

This time lag is a mixed blessing – on the one hand, it reduces
the effects of climate change and has prevented a more rapid and
severe warming than that observed to date. On the other hand, it
has perhaps helped to lull the public and politicians into compla-
cency, as the global warming underway is only partly noticeable

to us. The lag makes climate change more slow in setting in but it makes it also slow to respond to any countermeasures. If we stopped the further increase in atmospheric greenhouse gas concentrations this very minute, the global climate would still continue to warm by about 0.5 °C until the end of the century, as the ocean catches up with the warming and slowly stops taking up more heat.

Let us move on from heat storage to heat transport by the oceans. The oceans are not just a giant bucket full of water which passively stores heat. They play a very active and dynamic role for our climate due to their currents, which transport vast amounts of heat around the planet. Some heat is transported by the subtropical gyres and also by the smaller eddies in the ocean – as in the atmosphere, heat is generally transported from the equator to the poles, i.e. down the gradient from warm to cold. This helps to balance out the excess heat taken up in the tropics from the sun, as heat is emitted into space at higher latitudes.

More interesting, however, is the role of the thermohaline circulation discussed earlier, which transports large amounts of heat towards the sink areas in the North Atlantic and around the Arctic (see Fig. 1.4). In the Atlantic, this causes what climatologists call an "anomalous" heat transport: it is directed northward throughout the entire Atlantic, even in the southern hemisphere. This means that, in the South Atlantic, the thermohaline circulation transports heat towards the equator, i.e. up the gradient from cold to warm. This heat continues its path across the equator and further north, until released in the mid-to-high latitude North Atlantic. This large heat transport northward across the equator is the main reason why the northern hemisphere of our planet is warmer than the southern hemisphere. It is possible because the Atlantic Ocean is "sandwiched" between continents; this allows a vigorous north-south flow. Without this, as in the atmosphere, flow would tend to be aligned east-west with little exchange across the equator.

In the recent history of the Earth, this ocean circulation has proved to be quite unstable, switching its course and leading to some abrupt and dramatic climate changes. These are well-documented for the last great Ice Age, which took place between 100,000 and 10,000 years ago. For most of this time, the Atlantic circulation looked rather different than it does today. Data from sediment layers tell us that deep water formation did not occur in the Greenland-Norwegian Seas as it does today but, apparently, much further south: somewhere south of Iceland in the open Atlantic. Thus, the ocean did not transport heat up to the high latitudes, which is one reason for the bitter cold at these latitudes. However, every few thousand years, temperatures in Greenland jumped up by over 10°C within a few decades – not quite up to present-day temperatures for Greenland but, nevertheless, a major warming. This happened more than twenty times during the last 100,000 years and these events are called Dansgaard-Oeschger events, after the Danish scientist Willi Dansgaard and his Swiss colleague Hans Oeschger, who first described them.

The reason for these events was, apparently, a sudden initiation of deep water formation in the Nordic Seas and, as a consequence, a great northward push of warm and salty Atlantic waters. Sediment layers near Iceland show that salinity in the ocean suddenly increased whenever the temperatures in Greenland warmed. Furthermore, the most recent European ice coring effort in Antarctica (carried out as part of the EPICA project) showed that each time the temperatures jumped up in Greenland, they switched from a gradual warming trend to a gradual cooling trend in Antarctica. This is a clear indication of an increase in ocean heat transport in the Atlantic; model simulations of Dansgaard-Oeschger events show the same pattern.

There is also good evidence for a second kind of sudden ocean circulation change – a complete shutdown of deep-water formation in the North Atlantic. This has happened several times in the Earth's history, apparently in response to massive freshwater inflows into the North Atlantic. These freshwater inflows were either due to a major influx of continental ice (so-called Heinrich events, where huge iceberg armadas drifted across the Atlantic) or meltwater from melting ice at the end of the last Ice Age. For example, about 8200 years ago, an ice dam holding back a major meltwater lake on the North American continent, called Lake Agassiz, broke causing the last strong cooling event seen in the Greenland ice cores. A shutdown of the circulation also means cold events in Europe. Such events are documented from pollen data and sediment cores. This all makes physical sense – adding a large amount of freshwater to the Atlantic will form a veritable freshwater "lid," preventing the sinking of water and, thereby, stopping the deep-water formation which is critical for the thermohaline circulation.

In contrast to these cold climate phases at northern Atlantic latitudes, which have a clear cause, a particular interesting aspect of the warm Dansgaard-Oeschger events is that we are not able to find any sign of a large trigger for these ocean current changes in the data. We believe that some very small variation in climate, perhaps one of the weak solar cycles, was enough to trigger the oceanic change, because the ocean circulation was very unstable at the time – it must have been very close to a "critical" threshold, in other words, a threshold at which a major change could occur. This is no mere speculation – the physics of such critical thresholds is quite well understood. The cause is a very delicate balance in the salinity of the North Atlantic, specifically between the freshwater input from rain, rivers and meltwater, and the supply of additional salty water from the south through the ocean currents. As the flow depends on salinity (as we saw earlier) and salinity, in turn, depends on the flow, we have a classic positive feedback mechanism – something that every physicist will recognize as being conducive to unstable behavior and the potential to "flip" into a different state. Climate models have been used to systematically investigate this threshold behavior. In Chapter 4, we will discuss the risk of such instabilities in the ocean currents occuring again in the future. At this stage, we should keep in mind as a lesson from climate history that ocean currents can be quite unstable, and these instabilities can lead to major regional climate changes.

Even in the climate we are accustomed to, the dynamics of the oceans and the interplay between currents, winds and water temperatures have led to fluctuations. The most important of these fluctuations are known, respectively, as the El Niño phenomenon (also known as the *Southern Oscillation*) and the North Atlantic Oscillation. The name El Niño was originally given to a sudden warming of the ocean temperatures in the eastern tropical Pacific (off the coast of South America), which happens every three to seven years and lasts for months. Today, we know that this is the warm phase of a natural fluctuation, during the course of which the trade winds die down and warm water from the tropical *warm pool* (see above) "swashes" eastward from the western part of the Pacific. This, in turn, further accentuates the weakening of the trade winds (a classic positive feedback mechanism) and causes, for example, drought in Indonesia and Australia and increased rains in South America. Eventually, ocean waves running along the equator across the Pacific mark the end of this phenomenon – the system oscillates back and forth. By contrast, the North Atlantic Oscillation (NAO) is the result of a "see-saw" in the sea-level pressure between the Icelandic low and the Azores high, which is also influenced by ocean temperatures and determines whether we have mild and stormy winters with strong westerly winds over Europe (during the positive phases of the NAO) or whether we experience cold and dry winters (during the negative phases).

The third way the oceans influence climate is by providing water to the atmosphere through evaporation (see Plate 2 in the color section). Most people will be aware that the water that falls as rain or snow on land, ultimately, comes from the ocean (and will end up again in the ocean at the end of the water cycle). The amount of water moving about in this way is staggering: every year, over 400,000 km^3 of water evaporate from the oceans – that is about twenty times the amount of water in the Baltic Sea. On average, the air above the oceans is about 80% saturated with water vapor (i.e. it has a relative humidity of 80%). Water which evaporates from the ocean stays in the air for about ten days on average (that is, every ten days all the water in the atmosphere is replaced) and is transported about 1000 kilometers before it rains out again. Overall, however, the atmosphere contains surprisingly little water: if all the water were to rain out at once, this would raise sea levels by only 3 cm.

Water, of course, is the basis of clouds and changing cloud cover is one of very few ways in which the energy budget of the Earth and, thus, the global mean temperature of the Earth can be changed. Such a change can only be brought about through a change in incoming solar radiation (e.g. by variations in solar activity), by changing the portion of solar radiation that is reflected (the so-called albedo; this is where clouds have a big effect), or by changing the outgoing long-wave radiation. By providing ample water for clouds, the oceans have a cooling effect on climate.

What fewer people know is that the water cycle is also very closely connected to the energy cycle. Evaporating water uses up a lot of heat – the so-called latent heat of evaporation – as water vapor is in a higher energy state than liquid water. As soon as the water vapor condenses into droplets (i.e., when clouds form), this heat is released again. Evaporation is, thus, a heat sink at the sea surface and it consumes a large fraction of the sun's heat that arrives at the sea surface. Condensation up at cloud level represents the flip side of the coin: it is a great heat source for the atmosphere.

A special and important example of this connection is tropical storms: evaporation from the sea surface is their main energy source. This is why they do not occur over land (they die down very quickly after moving onto land) or over cold waters (where the evaporation rate is too low). In the centre of a hurricane, air saturated with water rises up and, as the pressure drops during the ascent, it cools and thereby becomes super-saturated. As a consequence, heat is released. The air parcel thereby becomes warmer than the ambient air and this makes it rise even faster. This results in a column of vigorously rising air and a resultant inflow of air to this region near the surface to feed the updraft. The high winds over the ocean accelerate evaporation which reinforces the energy supply to the storm. The Coriolis force deflects the winds trying to converge towards the centre of the storm and makes the hurricane spin: anticlockwise in the northern hemisphere, clockwise in the southern. Since the Coriolis force vanishes directly on the equator, no hurricanes are found there; they occur only at latitudes at least 5° north and south of the equator.

The fourth way in which oceans affect climate is through ice. As mentioned above, one way to influence the global heat budget is to change the albedo, i.e. the portion of sunlight which is reflected from the Earth or its atmosphere. A particularly effective way to do this is to change ocean water to ice or vice versa.

Sea water freezes at around -1.8 °C – the salt content acts as a mild anti-freeze. As we see on satellite images, ocean water belongs to the darkest surfaces on Earth, and it absorbs over 90% of the incoming solar radiation. Ice, on the other hand, belongs to the brightest surfaces, reflecting over 90%. This leads to a powerful influence of the oceans on climate: when polar regions become warmer and the sea ice cover shrinks, less sunlight is reflected and more is absorbed, amplifying the warming. (As will be discussed in Chapter 4, this is an important process which is at work right now in the Arctic and it is an important factor in explaining the particularly large warming seen in Arctic regions in recent decades.) However, the oceans do not only form sea-ice, they also supply water for snow on land and for the formation of glaciers and continental ice sheets, which provide a similar ice-albedo-feedback on land. At the height of the last Ice Age, 20,000 years ago, global sea levels were 120 meters lower than now – the difference in sea level from what we experience today represents how much water the oceans supplied to form the huge ice masses on land!

Finally, the fifth type of major oceanic influence on climate is through the exchange of gases with the atmosphere. The most important of these gases is carbon dioxide (CO_2). The atmosphere contains about 800 billion tons of carbon in the form of carbon dioxide (600 billion tons before human emissions started). If that sounds a lot, consider that the oceans contain about fifty times as much. This huge reservoir is coupled to the atmosphere: at the sea surface, the ocean can release gas to the atmosphere and also take up gas from the atmosphere. In this way, it in fact exchanges about 90 billion tons with the atmosphere each year. In the millennia before the industrial era, it took up about as much as it released and the system was in equilibrium. This can be seen from the ice core data, which show that the atmospheric concentration of carbon dioxide remained almost constant for thousands of years. Today, however, humans are emitting six billion tons of carbon per year to the atmosphere, of which about two billion end up in the ocean through gas exchange at the sea surface. As a result, the carbon dioxide content, not only of the atmosphere but also of the upper oceans, has been increasing, as documented through thousands of measurements. The fact that the ocean takes part of this burden is at the same time a blessing and a curse: although the oceanic uptake of atmospheric CO_2 reduces the effects of global warming by reducing the rate of atmospheric CO_2 increase (as we will discuss in Chapter 4), it on the other hand leads to an increasing acidification of the oceans (which we will discuss in Chapter 5).

2 Life in the Oceans

Life began in the oceans and, through time, the ocean has been home to countless fascinating and beautiful plants and animals. Although most of the organisms that have evolved and lived in the oceans throughout the history of the Earth have now become extinct, this is merely an expression of the fact that life is constantly changing and evolving. Today, a fantastic variety of organisms can be found in the world's oceans. Nobody knows exactly how many species the oceans provide a home for but it is estimated that the number may be as high as 10 million or more - and with only 300,000 of them recorded by science, many of these organisms have still not been seen by the human eye.

Life in the oceans and the system "Earth"

Life in the oceans has played and still plays a major role in shaping the system "Earth" as a whole, that is to say, the planet as we know it. Approximately 3.4 billion years ago, some of the tiny primitive plants found in the primeval ocean (which really were only photosynthesizing bacteria known as "cyanobacteria") developed a form of photosynthesis in which oxygen is produced as a by-product. Thanks to this development, around 21% of the atmosphere we experience today is made up of oxygen – a concentration which is high enough to allow the survival of multi-celled organisms such as ourselves. As if this wasn't enough, the production of oxygen by ocean plants also led ultimately to the development of an ozone layer in the stratosphere at an altitude of 15 to 50 kilometers, which filters the ultraviolet radiation from the sun and, thereby, makes it possible for living organisms to survive on land. Prior to the development of this ozone layer, life on Earth was only possible in the oceans, as water can also filter UV radiation. Consequently, in spite of the fact that they are so tiny that they cannot even be seen with the naked eye, it is to the cyanobacteria that we owe our very existence.

Considering how important ocean organisms have been for creating the environment upon which we depend, it seems odd that most people have only a very limited knowledge of or respect for nature in the ocean. Most people recognize that many human activities on land threaten nature by altering the living conditions or habitats upon which living organisms depend. For this reason, most countries have laws which restrict the location and extent of activities which are environmentally harmful. In addition, conservation areas are established where nature, or at least parts thereof, can develop more or less free from human intervention. Worldwide, an estimated 18 million km² of land area is subject to some level of nature conservation regulations. Although there is absolutely nothing to suggest that nature in the oceans is less important than nature on land or less deserving of protection, it is estimated that there are today only 1.9 million km² of ocean area where nature conservation regulations apply. In view of the fact that the area of the Earth's surface which is covered by ocean is over twice that covered by land, one can wonder why nature conservation efforts are so limited in the sea.

The answer, undoubtedly, lies in the fact that the ocean is a very foreign and inhospitable environment for us humans. If we were to be thrown into the ocean, in most cases, we would not survive for very long. We are, therefore, usually limited to observing the ocean from its periphery, which normally means that we are looking out *over* the ocean rather than into it and at the life it contains. We can stand on a ship and look down at the ocean but, again, we cannot see the nature it contains. Some people use diving equipment or submarines to delve deeper into the oceans themselves for limited periods of time but, even then, our senses do not allow us to see and appreciate most of the nature present in the ocean.

How life on land is different from life in the oceans

Consider for a moment what we see when we take a walk in a forest. Most obvious to us are the trees and plants and smaller animals like insects and birds. Occasionally, we may be fortunate enough to see a large animal, like a deer, a wild boar, or a fox. And if we are really lucky, we might even see one of the large predators at the top of the food chain: for example an eagle or a wolf. However, our overall impression of nature in the forest is that it is dominated by small organisms feeding either directly on plants or on the organisms that eat plants. Now let us move on to an open meadow and observe nature here. What do we see? Different plants and an entirely different fauna: different birds, a rabbit in the distance, a snake basking in the sun and the black beetles of the forest floor replaced by butterflies. Instinctively, we know that the reason nature looks and behaves differently in these two different environments is that we have different plants growing in each of these areas.

Now let us move to the oceans and observe nature there. We will just jump randomly in and find a spot that is representative for the whole. This means that we are a long way from the coast and our favorite beach. In fact, we cannot see any land at all. The ocean floor is hundreds if not thousands of meters below us. What do we see? Nothing. No plants, no insects, no small animals. If we wait long enough, an individual fish or a school of small fish may come by and, even (very) occasionally, a larger fish which feeds upon smaller fish or a mammal such as a seal or whale may swim past. As a result, when asked to describe how they see nature in the open ocean, most people only conjure up images of fish, sharks and whales – but not the ecosystems that support them.

We have an intuitive understanding of nature on land and the factors which combine to structure the ecosystems there. We appreciate that, to a large extent, the range of plants on offer controls which types of herbivores are present, and we understand what makes up the rest of the ecosystem. We recognize also that the major challenges for the survival of plants are gaining access to water, light and nutrients. This is why plants on land often have huge root networks. Many grow very tall in order to reach more light. To do this, it has been necessary to develop strong stems or trunks capable of transporting water right to the top of the plant. Being large and multi-celled – with different cells which carry out different functions for the plant (water transport, reinforcement of cell walls, photosynthesis etc.) – gives plants a competitive advantage on land, where there is often a separation between water, which is found deep in the soil, and light which is found in abundance above the Earth's surface.

For ocean plants, access to water is no problem. Therefore, there is no need for the relatively large and differentiated forms typically associated with higher-developed land plants. In fact, it can also be argued that being a large plant in the open ocean would be a competitive disadvantage for the plants because they would sink and, thus, quickly end up in depths where barely any

light is available. Accordingly, most ocean plants are relatively
small: 95% or more of the photosynthesis taking place in the
ocean is carried out by plants which are too small to be discerned
by the naked eye – and there is just as much plant activity (photosynthesis) in the oceans as there is on land.

Ocean plants: phytoplankton

Collectively, these tiny plants are called phytoplankton: *phyto*
comes from Greek and means plant, while *plankton* is defined
as an organism which is too small or weak to control its own
position in the presence of water movements. Because we cannot
see phytoplankton, we tend not to appreciate the fact that these
organisms are comprised of a number of different taxonomic
groups, and that the characteristics of these groups are very different. In addition there are, relatively speaking, huge size differences between the different phytoplankton species. All are, of
course, very small in relation to us, but the relative difference in
size between the largest and the smallest types of phytoplankton
is actually greater than the relative difference between a mouse
and an elephant. Nobody would argue that mice and elephants
contribute in the same way to food chains on land and, of course,
to the animals that eat them, the size differences between different species of phytoplankton are hugely important (see Plate 5
in the color section).

Figure 2.1 The plankton food chain
Small phytoplankton is eaten by small zooplankton (small animals found in the
currents). Larger phytoplankton is eaten by large zooplankton that can directly
serve as nutrition for fish larvae. Where large phytoplankton is predominant,
the food chain is, therefore, very short and efficient and the number of fish is
generally high.

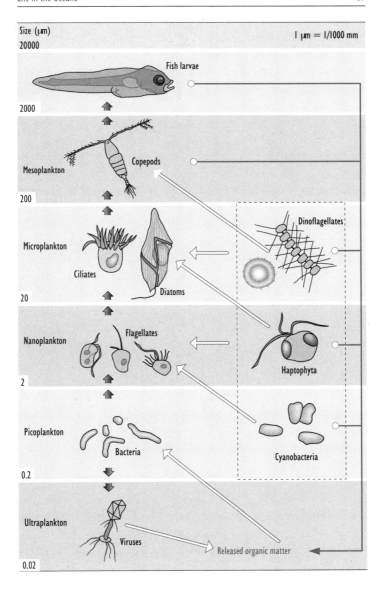

Size (μm)
20000

1 μm = 1/1000 mm

Fish larvae

2000

Mesoplankton

Copepods

200

Microplankton

Dinoflagellates

Ciliates

Diatoms

20

Nanoplankton

Flagellates

Haptophyta

2

Picoplankton

Bacteria

Cyanobacteria

0.2

Ultraplankton

Viruses

Released organic matter

0.02

Large phytoplankton cells with a cell length of more than 20 μm (1 μm = 0.001 mm) can be directly consumed by the largest of the animal plankton ("zooplankton"), and the large zooplankton can be directly consumed by fish larvae or small fish. Some small fish also feed directly on large phytoplankton (Fig. 2.1).

Thus, when phytoplankton communities are dominated by large species, there are only one or two links or steps in the food chain before the energy captured from sunlight through the process of photosynthesis reaches the level of the fish. Every time energy is transferred from one level to another in the food chain (i.e. when a small animal eats a plant or when a larger animal eats the animal that ate the plant – these levels are known as "trophic levels") around 90% of the energy contained in the organism being eaten is lost. Consequently, short food chains, i.e. those dominated by large phytoplankton cells, are most efficient at transferring energy from primary producers (phytoplankton) to fish. We predict, therefore, that regions with predominantly large phytoplankton will also be more productive with respect to the volume of fish they contain than regions dominated by small phytoplankton, and this is indeed the case: in temperate regions, where large phytoplankton can be over-abundant at times, fisheries' yields (amount of fish brought in per unit effort) are much greater than in tropical regions where small phytoplankton species almost always dominate.

What determines whether it is large or small species of phytoplankton that dominate in a particular region? The answer is simple: nutrient availability. Plants need water, nutrients and light in order to grow. Water is no problem for ocean organisms, but finding both nutrients and light in abundant supply is a challenge. The uptake of nutrients by phytoplankton is an energy-intensive process which takes place through the cell wall. Being small is an advantage in environments with limited nutrient availability, because small cells have a greater surface area to volume ratio than large cells. Consequently, smaller phytoplankton cells tend to dominate wherever nutrients are scarce.

In the open ocean, the availability of nitrogen (N) is a limiting factor for plant activity, although in some coastal areas it is phosphorus (P) which periodically limits activity. In recent years, it has also become clear that, in large parts of the southern Pacific Ocean, the concentration of iron (Fe) regulates phytoplankton activity. This is a particularly interesting observation, as it allows us to understand why the oxygen in the atmosphere did not develop uniformly throughout the Earth's history. As a consequence of volcanic activity, iron dust is delivered into the ocean, where it can stimulate photosynthesis and, therefore, the production of oxygen in areas of otherwise limited iron availability.

Gaining access to light is a challenge for phytoplankton because light in the ocean is supplied by the sun. This means, of course, that light is only abundant in the very upper layers of the ocean. With increasing depth, the available light is attenuated exponentially. The rate of light reduction is dependent upon how clear the water is. In regions where the surface waters contain large amounts of nutrients and there is an abundance of phytoplankton, light does not penetrate deeply into the water column. As a rule of thumb, we say that phytoplankton growth is possible in the water column down to the depth at which 1% of the sunlight entering the water column is still present. In ocean waters with a high nutrient concentration in surface waters (i.e. in certain seasons in temperate regions), this means that phytoplankton growth may only be possible in the upper 10–20 meters. By contrast, where nutrient availability is very limited, such as in most tropical waters, photosynthesis may still be possible at a depth of 100 meters or more.

We know from our house and garden plants that some species

thrive in full light while others prefer less light. The same is true for the phytoplankton. In relatively stable water columns, i.e. those in which the water is not well mixed from top to bottom, the distribution of species in the phytoplankton community can be very different as we move from the brighter light in the surface waters to the darker conditions further down in the water column. Thus, as for land plants, there is a specific range of light intensities within which a given species can survive. In a well mixed water column, phytoplankton are transported throughout the entire water column. Thus, they must be able to tolerate both high and low light intensities. However, if the water column is stratified, i.e. if it comprises different water masses which are layered one above the other, it is possible for phytoplankton to "select" the light conditions to which they are best suited. Many of the phytoplankton species found in stratified water have flagella which allow them to swim, and therefore position themselves in a stable water column.

We see, then, that sufficient light for photosynthesis is found at the surface of the ocean. In the process of photosynthesis, the nutrients found in the surface waters become incorporated in the organic particles of the phytoplankton and subsequently make their way into the organisms that feed on them. These nutrient-containing particles weigh more than water and, thus, sink out of the surface layer. When they sink, they take the nutrients they contain with them into the deeper layers of the ocean. We can see by measuring temperature or salinity in the water column that, over most of the Earth's ocean area, the water column is not mixed. In other words, there are two or more different water masses layered one above the other. As these water masses have different temperatures and salinities, they also have different densities. Thus, just like oil and vinegar in salad dressing, they do not readily mix without an input of energy into the system.

If there was no mixing of nutrient-rich water from the lower layers of the ocean with the surface waters then the oceans would be devoid not only of phytoplankton but also of all the organisms which depend on phytoplankton for their survival. Fortunately, there are mechanisms which can transport nutrients from deep to surface waters (see Chapter 1). Upwelling of deep waters to the surface occurs along westerly coasts (for example along the African and South American coasts), where the interplay between different physical processes often causes surface waters to be pushed away from the coast. Deep water then moves up to replace this surface water. Upwelling of nutrient-rich deep water also occurs at the equator where, due to the rotation of the Earth and resulting Coriolis force, the surface waters of the two hemispheres flow in opposite directions away from each other (see Chapter 1). As well as in these two equatorial and coastal upwelling systems, major upwelling also takes place near Antarctica. The stimulation of phytoplankton growth caused by major upwelling systems as a result of the transportation of nutrients towards surface waters can be clearly seen in the geographic distribution of the photosynthetic pigment chlorophyll (an indicator of the amount of phytoplankton) in surface waters (see Plate 4 in the color section).

Localized upwelling of deep water can also occur due to the presence of small hills in the ocean floor and/or local wind conditions. Such small-scale upwelling can give rise to a "patchy" distribution of phytoplankton. In other words, thanks to the localized physical conditions that allow nutrients to be transported from deep to surface waters in certain areas, the horizontal distribution of phytoplankton throughout the ocean is not even. In some cases, dramatic differences in phytoplankton abundance can be seen on a scale of only a few hundred meters. As we saw above, the vertical distribution of phytoplankton in the well-lit

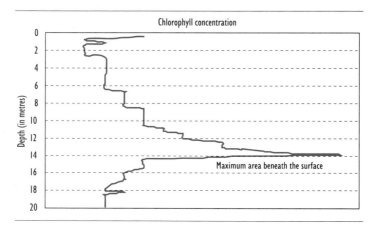

Figure 2.2 The distribution of the chlorophyll (phytoplankton) in the
          water columns shows that plant life in the ocean is not
          uniform

regions of the water column is also not necessarily homogeneous. Often, a fairly low concentration of phytoplankton can be
found right at the top. This can be due to a shortage of nutrients
at the surface or to levels of light or ultraviolet radiation being
so extreme at the surface as to be damaging to the phytoplankton cells. In these cases, there is often an area further down in
the water column where the phytoplankton concentration peaks.
Frequently, such peaks are located at the interface between two
water masses and, occasionally, they are very narrow, covering a
vertical distance of only a few meters or even less.

    Small-scale sampling of subsurface phytoplankton communi-
ties has demonstrated that, within the peaks themselves, there
can be a distinct distribution of each species of phytoplankton.
Some decrease in concentration with increasing depth. Others
increase. Some are only found in a very narrow strip, while others

may be spread throughout the entire range. Some species are only found in association with other species, while some never occur with certain species. What this shows us is that, while our sensory systems do not allow us to recognize different habitats in, for example, a two-meter thick layer of the water column, the phytoplankton can – and they exploit these different habitats.

Generally, in ecology, it is believed that the number of species found in any given ecosystem is limited by the number of "niches" (different habitats) found in the ecosystem. Therefore, it has long been a mystery for ecologists how there can be so many different phytoplankton species when, seen through our eyes, there are so few different niches to be occupied in the surface waters of the ocean. In 1961, Evelyn Hutchinson described the fact that there are many different species in a seemingly homogeneous environment as the "paradox of the plankton." Today, we realize that the world that phytoplankton inhabit is not nearly as homogeneous as our senses lead us to believe. What is simply cold and wet to us presents many different living conditions for the phytoplankton. Phytoplankton organisms are too small to be seen with the naked eye, but they are still able to appreciate and exploit small-scale differences in ocean habitats which are also invisible to us. Thus, it is very difficult to research the diversity of these species. To date, we have still not developed the necessary investigative methods that would allow us to fully appreciate the small-scale heterogeneity in living conditions and the distribution of ocean plants.

The evolution of phytoplankton

Not only is it very difficult to quantify the small-scale distribution of these tiny plants, but we are also only just beginning to appreciate how very different they are from one another. In fact, from a genetic point of view the phytoplankton species are more different from each other than land plants.

The molecular methods developed in recent years allow us to trace the evolutionary roots of these organisms, and they indicate that a fascinating mechanism is responsible for the evolution of the different phytoplankton groups: it would appear that some primitive non-photosynthesizing organisms "ingested" cells of the primitive photosynthetic cyanobacteria. The host organism and the cyanobacterium entered into a symbiotic relationship with mutual benefits for both organisms. Presumably, the cyanobacterium received protection and nutrients from the host cell and the host cell received energy from the photosynthesis of the cyanobacteria. Eventually, the relationship became permanent and a new organism evolved. This process repeated itself many times with different hosts and ingested organisms and, ultimately, led to the many different groups of phytoplankton we know today.

Interestingly, there are still some organisms which are classified as belonging to specific groups of phytoplankton even though they are, actually, not true plants in the sense that they do not contain chlorophyll and do not photosynthesize. They are included in these phytoplankton groups because they share morphological and genetic characteristics with them and are, therefore, more similar to their photosynthesizing relatives in these groups than to any other group of organisms. As they lack chloroplasts and thus the ability to photosynthesize, they must obtain energy from other sources.

There are a number of different feeding strategies that such non-photosynthesizing phytoplankton have developed. Some swallow their prey whole and then digest them. A special variant of this form of feeding has recently been discovered in a number of species, whereby the feeding organism does not destroy the chloroplasts in the phytoplankton cells it ingests. The rest of the cell is broken down and digested but the chloroplasts remain unharmed; the host cell uses the energy produced by the chloroplasts via photosynthesis until they die.

It would be tempting to speculate whether we might be witnessing evolution in action here. Is this the start of a relationship between predator and prey that, conceivably, could become more permanent over time? And what is it that signals to the host cell that it should not destroy and digest the chloroplasts of the photosynthesizing cells it consumes? How does the cell "know" that it might be beneficial to retain the chloroplast? No one knows the answers to these questions yet. However, understanding the inter- and intracellular communication mechanisms in such organisms could have far-reaching consequences for example in the treatment of diseases and the development of nanotechnology.

The oceans – a dangerous place to live

The world of plants in the oceans displays a fantastic variety of forms and modes of life. However, all of these organisms share a common difference to land plants which is worthy of closer consideration: they are all very small – and most consist of only of a single cell. As a consequence, they are all exceedingly vulnerable to predation: one bite and the entire plant ceases to exist.

Many phytoplankton species have shapes that are difficult to reconcile with what might be expected of "normal" plant functions, such as the capture of nutrients and light or carrying out photosynthesis. These unique morphological features include spine-like protrusions of the cell wall, protective armoring made of silica or calcium carbonate, and chain-like formations or elongated cells which make it difficult for a predator to devour the entire cell.

Other phytoplankton species produce toxins which also seem to reduce the risk of being preyed upon. For a long time, it was debated whether or not toxin production could be a strategy to reduce the risk of predation on single-celled organisms. Those who argued against this possibility pointed out that once a cell has been ingested, it makes precious little difference to the cell whether or not its consumer becomes ill or dies as a result. However, it has now been shown that the toxins released from some phytoplankton cells to the surrounding waters cause the tiny animals that eat these phytoplankton to swim erratically and even backwards! Apparently, the toxin causes the potential predators of the phytoplankton to lose control over their movements. Of course, this makes it difficult to catch prey, so the production of toxins can therefore help even a single-celled organism to avoid predation.

Clearly, avoiding predation is the biggest challenge for the tiny plants in the ocean. In fact, predation is believed to be one of the primary forces structuring the shape of all ecosystems in the ocean – after all, phytoplankton are not the only organisms to have evolved defense mechanisms against predation.

It is interesting how many of the small animals (zooplankton) living in the ocean resemble shrimp, even though there is no close evolutionary relationship between these species

This can, perhaps, be explained by considering the most obvious and important feature in a shrimp: namely its tail, which is nothing more than a muscle used for "jumping" through the water. In other words, a shrimp (and all of the other organisms which resemble it) is almost entirely comprised of a highly developed escape mechanism which can be brought into play when the organism senses a potential predator. The fact that so many marine organisms possess this type of tail indicates that having such an escape mechanism must offer a survival advantage for life in the ocean.

Another example which gives an indication of the level of threat of predation in the ocean comes from the examination of the reproductive strategies of marine organisms. Investing reproductive energy wisely is a trade-off between producing a very large number of offspring in order to maximize the chances of some offspring surviving long enough to be able to reproduce themselves, and also equipping each of the offspring with enough energy resources to be able to optimise their chances of survival. With the exception of the marine mammals, evolution in the ocean appears to have favored animals which invest their reproductive energy in producing very many eggs or young rather than those which produce few but well-nurtured young.

This can be illustrated by considering a female cod: in order to ensure the continuation of the population, a mother cod needs only to have two (actually just less than two, as cod males mate with more than one female) of the offspring she produces in her lifetime to survive to adulthood. How many eggs does she produce in her reproductive lifetime? If we assume that she is not fished out of the ocean but lives out her full life expectancy, then she will lay on the order of 10 million eggs. Just imagine if a land animal the size of a large cod needed to produce this many young in order to ensure the survival of the species.

Clearly, survival is a challenge for small ocean-dwelling organisms and one of the major factors contributing to this challenge is predation. Another is finding food (which, for the prey organism involved, is simply a matter of predation again!).

Life in the ocean lives by different rules than life on land

The fact that predation appears to be the major defining factor for the structure of ocean ecosystems underlines an important difference between nature in the ocean and nature on land. On land, gaining access to water is instrumental in structuring most ecosystems. Access to water is not a problem for marine ecosystems. Thus, life in the ocean is based on different basic premises than life on land.

For many reasons, we can be thankful that this is the case. Consider, for example, the fact that on land plants will grow wherever that there is light and water. If the same were true in the oceans, the immediate surface layer would be a thick and oily foam of phytoplankton. This layer would effectively form a "lid" on the ocean, resulting in greatly reduced rates of evaporation from the ocean compared to the evaporation we actually see. Reduced evaporation would lead to less rainfall and a much less hospitable climate than the one we – and all the other organisms dwelling in the drier regions of the Earth – require to survive. It is, therefore, clearly an advantage for land-dwelling organisms that the basic premises for life in the oceans are different from those for life on land.

The fact that nature has different ground rules in the ocean than those that govern life on land only increases our difficulty in understanding and protecting nature in the ocean. In our society's attempts to regulate human intervention into life in the oceans, we tend to assume that the lessons learned about nature and nature conservation on land will also apply in the oceans. This is, however, not necessarily the case.

The most obvious direct interaction between human activity and nature in the ocean is through fishing which, in essence, is simply a form of predation. We have just learned that predation is a major structuring factor for ocean ecosystems. With that understanding, we can predict that fishing is likely to have a significant influence on these ecosystem structures and – as we will see in Chapter 6 – scientists are now beginning to realize that this is indeed the case.

Interactions between organisms and the ocean: *Calanus finmarchicus*

The focus of this chapter until now has been the diversity of life in the oceans and the interactions between the organisms found there. However, not even a very short introduction to life in the ocean such as the one presented here can be complete without emphasizing the importance of interactions between organisms living in the ocean and the ocean itself.

Almost everyone has heard of the migrations undertaken for example by salmon, during which the adult fish swim upstream into freshwater rivers and streams to spawn, and the young then allow themselves to be carried back to the open ocean where they feed and mature. However, when the time comes to mate and produce their own offspring, they are able to find their way back to the very same river from which they emerged as a juvenile, in order to complete their life cycle. This example again underlines how life in the ocean is able to differentiate, to a much greater degree than we on land, between different water masses, and to navigate within and between them.

This ability to identify different water masses and to use the prevailing currents is not, however, confined to large ocean animals such as fish. One of the most fascinating examples of how ocean organisms exploit conditions in the ocean in order to complete their life cycles involves a tiny copepod, *Calanus finmarchicus* (see Plate 6 in the color section).

This animal, which is about the size of the eye of a sewing needle, is one of the most important prey organisms for fish larvae in the North Atlantic. For example, it has been demonstrated that the survival of young cod in the North Sea is related to the availability of these *Calanus*. More *Calanus* means more food being available to the baby cod, and this leads to a greater rate of survival to adulthood. This means, of course, that the predation pressure on *Calanus* is enormous. Reproduction in this species occurs via egg-laying and is dependent upon the adult individuals being able to feed on large quantities of phytoplankton. When phytoplankton are abundant in the North Sea during summertime, this species has no problem reproducing itself, and it can replace the young that are eaten by hungry predators. However, the situation is less straightforward during the winter, when the water column is well mixed due to winter storms. As a result of this mixing, the phytoplankton are continuously being transported from the surface to the bottom of the water column. This, combined with the fact that days are shorter and the sun less strong than during summer, means that the average light conditions are not sufficient to support substantial photosynthesis and the phytoplankton growth it supports. This means that there is insufficient food for *Calanus* to produce eggs.

Nevertheless, the potential grazers of *Calanus* remain in the North Sea during the winter months and they are hungry! Accordingly, if the *Calanus* population stayed in the North Sea during the winter, it would be at risk of being eaten out of existence. Presumably for this reason, the animal has evolved a life cycle in which it leaves the North Sea during the winter months. The juvenile *Calanus* hatched in the North Sea during the summer have "learned" (i.e. have genetically evolved) to ride the prevailing currents in order to be transported off of the

Continental Shelf and into the open North Atlantic during late summer/autumn.

Some, as yet unidentified, cue then causes the nearly mature individuals to descend in the water column to depths of up to about 1000 meters, where the animals go into "diapause," which is a form of hibernation. It has emerged that the animals are not randomly distributed at depth in the North Atlantic during winter but are concentrated in specific water masses. The population of *Calanus* which comes from the North Sea primarily hibernates in a body of water in the Faroe-Shetland Channel which is particularly cold (zero or less as saltwater freezes at a lower temperature than freshwater). Hibernating in very cold water is an advantage, as metabolic activity is reduced. This is also why hibernation in land-dwelling animals depends upon the temperature.

After several months in the cold, dark depths of the North Atlantic, the males awaken from their diapause and begin their ascent towards the surface. They stop after about forty days at a depth of about 300 meters and wait for their mates to arrive. Moving 700 meters up in the water column may not sound like a very great distance but it is important to remember how tiny these animals are. For these organisms, traveling a distance of 700 meters would be the equivalent of us of traveling about 500 kilometers. Imagine sitting down about 500 kilometers away from your partner and waiting for him or her to find you!

Clearly, making contact between mates is a challenge for these organisms but nature has also devised a mechanism which helps to shift the balance in their favor. While waiting, the male "dances" in the water and leaves a potent chemical trail behind him which makes the job of finding a mate much easier for the ascending females. Once mating has taken place, both males and females ascend to the surface.

When the females reach the surface, they lay as many eggs as they can with the energy reserves they have managed to store all winter in little fat globules.

This, of course, is why it was so important that they hibernated in a very cold place. The cold temperature slowed the pace of all the body processes that wanted a piece of the energy cake. It was also important that the long sleep took place in a very dark place, as the world is a dangerous place for a copepod with a predator waiting to feed lurking around every corner. When these animals hibernate, the safest place to do so is in the dark, where they cannot be seen. It also helps if this place is one where there are not a lot of hungry mouths around. Thus, hibernation takes place under ideal conditions to ensure the survival of the species.

How many eggs does a *Calanus* female lay when she reaches the surface? Probably as many as she can given the energy she has managed to hoard but certainly no more than about 100. You might think that the story (and the long travels of this little organism) ends here. However, survival of the species is still far from assured at this point. That is because these eggs have been laid in a place where there is no food for the offspring (nauplii larvae) which will eventually hatch out of these eggs. Somehow, the eggs need to be transported to a region where there will be food available when they release the precious cargo they contain. Why didn't the female *Calanus* simply wait to lay her eggs until she had arrived at the feeding grounds herself? Again, the answer is probably found in the constant threat of predation. Given how dangerous the world is for a copepod, the chances of a given female's genes reaching the feeding grounds (that are still hundreds of real kilometers away) are much better if they are packed into 100 different packages (i.e. 100 eggs) rather than into just one (i.e. the female copepod).

Of course, eggs cannot swim on their own but the reason that the parent *Calanus* expended so much time and energy to get to where they did to produce their offspring was that they could ensure that, by releasing their eggs at this particular time and in this particular place, the eggs could hitch a free ride to rich feeding grounds in the North Sea. The prevailing currents are such that eggs released in exactly this region are transported first towards the north and, later, into shelf sea waters, where phyto-plankton growth is abundant and there will be plenty to eat for the emerging *Calanus* offspring.

Evolution has been busy perfecting this intricate interaction between processes in the physical environment (in this case the prevailing current system) and the life cycle of *Calanus finmarchicus* and has created a masterpiece. While fascinating, this type of life history is, however, by no means unique. Ocean organisms have evolved to exploit the environment in which they live and they are part of a complicated system full of ingenious twists which we humans have only a limited under-standing and appreciation of. The story of *Calanus finmarchicus* is also interesting because it emphasizes how hopelessly inadequate our understanding is of how climate change may affect ocean processes.

The currents that the copepods use as their transport to and from their overwintering grounds are influenced by the North Atlantic Current, i.e. the warm surface waters travelling north to replace the bottom water formed in the Greenland and Lab-rador Seas (see Chapter 1). Likewise, the cold deep water upon which *Calanus* depends in order to hibernate originates in the Norwegian Sea. How much of this cold deep water reaches the Faroe-Shetland Channel also depends upon oceanographic phe-nomena, which are potentially influenced by climate change.

A marked decrease in the size of the *Calanus finmarchicus*

population in the North Sea has been recorded since the 1960s, and this decrease can largely be explained by two different factors: a change in the direction of the prevailing winds during late winter/early spring (which reduces the likelihood of *Calanus* being transported into the North Sea after having arisen from the deep waters in the Faroe-Shetland Channel) and a reduction in the amount of deep Norwegian Sea water reaching the Faroe-Shetland Channel (which represents a reduction in size of the overwintering habitat of *Calanus*). Both the change in prevailing wind patterns and the amount of deep Norwegian Sea water in the Faroe-Shetland Channel can be related to climate changes during the last approximately 50 years.

At this point, however, it is not possible to establish the cause of these changes but what this example shows us is that changes in climate will have consequences for biological communities and ecosystem functions. Thus, seemingly unrelated phenomena, such as the amount of cold deep Norwegian Sea water in the Faroe-Shetland Channel and the survival of cod in the North Sea, can in fact be linked.

The ocean as a system

This example dramatically illustrates that the ocean is a complex system in which the organisms it contains are linked to one another and to their environment in complex and intricate ways. We still lack an understanding of how all of these interactions work. However, we are beginning to recognize that the features of the ocean system are interwoven in such a way that a change in one part of the system can have unexpected consequences in another part of the system. We are also beginning to realize that abrupt changes can occur that alter the entire system. For a succinct comparison, we could liken the ocean system to a camel: the system is very robust and can tolerate a great deal of change and pressure – but only up to a certain point. Like the camel's back that breaks when the last straw is placed upon it, sub-components of the ocean system can also collapse. Examples of such sub-components could be specific fisheries, habitats in bays or estuaries, or coral reef systems. Once the final straw has been added and the camel's back broken, it is not simply a case of removing the last straw in order to get the animal back on its feet again. Although it may be possible to get the camel back up again, it will be very expensive to heal its back, and the back will never be as strong as it was before it was broken. Just like the analogy with the camel's back, it is clearly in the best interest of our society to manage human interactions with the ocean and the life it contains in such a manner as to ensure that sub-components of the system do not collapse.

Human interactions with the ocean and the life it contains are extensive and becoming more so every day. In the following chapters, these interactions are described along with their documented and potential impacts on various sub-components of the ocean system. Only through a better understanding of interactions within the ocean system itself and the impact of human activities on the system, will it be possible to develop wise management practices to govern our interactions with the ocean.

3 Global Element Cycles

In the closing paragraphs of Chapter 1, it was noted that gas exchange takes place between the atmosphere and the ocean. Occasionally, our senses are able to detect (but not quantify) this exchange. Usually, it is our sense of smell which tells us that an exchange is taking place. This happens, for example, when particular phytoplankton species "bloom," i.e. their active growth results in an accumulation of large concentrations. As these species release sulfur compounds, the air near the phytoplankton bloom can take on a characteristic smell which is not dissimilar to rotten eggs. We are able to smell the bloom because gases are released from the ocean to the air. Our senses can also detect the release of gases from the ocean when phytoplankton containing certain toxins bloom.

At this point it is appropriate to mention toxin production in phytoplankton. Often, when a toxic phytoplankton bloom occurs, it makes media headlines and is treated as being a sign of a polluted or even dying ocean. Just as there are a number of poisonous plants on land, some phytoplankton species also contain toxins. However, it has been estimated that only about 1 % of the known phytoplankton species have this characteristic; it is also known that there are several different types of toxins involved.

One chemical group of toxins, generically known as "brevetoxins," can be released from the water to the air and, when inhaled, can irritate the human respiratory system. Unfortunately, the phytoplankton which produces this type of toxin is relatively abundant around, for example, the Florida (USA) coast, where many elderly people live. As the elderly often suffer from weakened respiratory systems, the release of brevetoxins to the atmosphere can be a serious public health problem here.

Although in cases like this, it is possible for us to sense the gas exchange occurring between the ocean and the atmosphere, these examples are the exception rather than the rule – normal gas exchange takes place continuously without us being able to sense it. As the oceans cover 71% of the Earth's surface, this exchange has a tremendous quantitative impact on the global cycles of several elements. It has already been emphasized in Chapter 2 that our interest in the exchange of gases between the oceans and the atmosphere is not merely academic. In that chapter, we looked at how the levels of oxygen in the atmosphere have increased during the history of the Earth – and, of course, that the bulk of this oxygen, at least initially, was created through photosynthesis in the ocean.

It is, however, not only oxygen which is exchanged between the atmosphere and the oceans. The exchange across this interface is also quantitatively important for the global cycling of elements such as carbon (C), nitrogen (N) and sulfur (S). In terms of the future of the oceans and the role they will play for global climate change, it is precisely the exchange of these three elements which is so important. Of these, carbon has received the most attention so far.

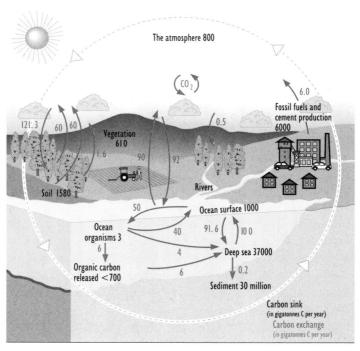

Figure 3.1 Diagram of global CO_2 cycle
Several points are noteworthy. 1. The largest carbon reservoirs are found in the sediment on the ocean bed. 2. In contrast to the land, the ocean absorbs more CO_2 than it releases. There is fifty times more carbon in the seawater than in the atmosphere.

Carbon

Fig. 3.1 shows a schematic representation of the global carbon cycle, which reveals several interesting features. To start with, let us examine the differences between the relative contributions of the land and the oceans to this cycle as a whole and, in particular, to the CO_2 concentration in the atmosphere. The most obvious difference is that the land gives off more CO_2 than it absorbs, while the ocean takes up more CO_2 than it releases to the atmosphere. Consequently, we describe the ocean as a "sink" for CO_2, while the land represents a "source" with respect to the atmosphere. The land has not always been the overly dominant source of CO_2 that it is today. However, human activities – and, more than anything else, the combustion of fossil fuels and the clearing of the photosynthesizing plant cover over large regions of the Earth – have distorted the ratio of CO_2 uptake/release to the extent that substantially more CO_2 is released to the atmosphere than is taken up. (On the subject of clearing, the amount of land on Earth now used for agriculture is approximately equivalent to the area of South America and the area of land used for grazing of farm animals is approximately equal to the area of Africa.)

The situation is different in the oceans, where more CO_2 is absorbed from the atmosphere than is released. Quantitatively, it appears that there is slightly more uptake of CO_2 in the oceans than on land, although this is very difficult to measure, particularly over the oceans. It is probably most correct to say that both land and the oceans take up approximately the same amounts of CO_2.

Another important difference between the land and ocean in the carbon cycle is that there is comparatively little carbon bound up in ocean fauna and flora in comparison to the land. The explanation for this is to be found largely in the differences in size between land and ocean plants (as discussed in Chapter 2), as well as the differences in size between the organisms which feed on these plants in the two different environments. It is, however, interesting to note that the absolute magnitude of photosynthesis in the oceans almost matches that on land, despite the smaller biomass. This illustrates that the "turnover" of the tiny plants in the ocean – i.e. their relative activity taking into account biomass – is much faster than that of the plants on land. As we are able to see the plants on land, we can recognize the role they play via photosynthesis in the carbon cycle. This is one of the reasons why there is so much environmental concern regarding the felling of rainforests. However, if we compare activity to biomass, it is the tiny ocean plants which are really effective at re-circulating carbon.

As already mentioned in the first chapter, the absolute amount of carbon in the ocean water (the so-called "pelagic region") is about fifty times greater than the amount of carbon in the atmosphere. If we now consider the continuous exchange of CO_2 between the oceans and the atmosphere, it becomes clear that predicting future atmospheric CO_2 concentrations requires not only an understanding of the amount of CO_2 released to the atmosphere, but also an understanding of how much makes it into the ocean – and how much stays there. As a result, considerable research effort is currently being devoted to understanding the processes that determine carbon uptake and retention ("sequestration") in the ocean.

Before taking a closer look at a handful of processes which determine the net uptake of carbon in the oceans, it is worth considering the tremendous amount of carbon which is found at the bottom of the ocean in the seabed. This reservoir, which is estimated to be in the order of 30 million gigatons, comprises by far the largest concentration of carbon anywhere on Earth. In order to understand the processes in the ocean which contribute to the ocean's ability to sequester carbon, it is worth considering for a moment how all of this carbon got to the bottom of the ocean and became incorporated in the sediment.

Of course, most of it originates from organic material (usually dead plants and animals) that has fallen to the ocean floor. Even though most organisms in the ocean are very small, it almost goes without saying that most of the carbon bound up in the ocean floor originated from the tiny phytoplankton and zooplankton introduced in the last chapter. However, not all of these organisms contribute equally to the deposition of carbon on the ocean floor

We focus first on the phytoplankton, as the majority of these organisms can remove carbon from their surrounding environment. They do so in the same way as all other so-called true plants – i.e. those plants which contain chloroplasts and carry out photosynthesis. During photosynthesis, CO_2 is converted with the aid of water and sunlight to the sugars which form the building blocks of living cells. During this process, oxygen (O_2) is released. All photosynthesizing plants contribute to the global carbon cycle (and to the nitrogen and oxygen cycles) but there is no guarantee that the carbon incorporated into particulate material via photosynthesis will fall to the bottom of the ocean. In fact, quite the opposite is the case, as most of the carbon bound by photosynthesis is broken down again in the surface layer of the ocean (see Fig. 3.2). In order to gain energy for growth and reproduction, the phytoplankton break down the sugar compounds again in which carbon is bound – so, in practice, the sugar acts simply as an interim store for most of the solar energy gained through photosynthesis.

The biological pump

During the breakdown of these sugars, CO_2 is released. If it is not the phytoplankton themselves which "breathe out" or respire the CO_2 again, this process can be carried out by the organisms in the food chain which have eaten the phytoplankton, or bacteria which decompose dead organic material and release the CO_2 bound by photosynthesis back into the surface waters of the ocean.

As surface waters are always in contact with the atmosphere, the CO_2 they contain can be quickly transferred to the atmosphere again. This means that the bulk of CO_2 bound via photosynthesis in the ocean is really only on a short visit there – it can return to, first, the surface waters and, then, the atmosphere within a narrow time-frame which makes this short-term retention of carbon in the oceans irrelevant in terms of the ocean's role in the net uptake of CO_2 from the atmosphere. What is much more important in this respect is the amount of organic material (or carbon) which is bound through photosynthesis in the upper layers of the ocean and then transported to the deep layers of the water column. This carbon is interesting because the surface and bottom layers of the water column do not normally mix (see Chapter 2). This means that the carbon "trapped" in the deepest water layers of the ocean does not come into direct contact with the atmosphere. Without such contact, it is practically impossible for this CO_2 to be exchanged with the atmosphere. This means that, for the purpose of timescales which are relevant for predicting future atmospheric CO_2 concentrations and therefore the climate, this CO_2 can be disregarded. This transport of organic material to the deep bottom waters of the ocean is known as the "biological pump," as it is biological processes (together with sinking due to gravity, of course) which are responsible for removing CO_2 from surface waters and delivering it to bottom waters.

This makes it critical to understand and quantify the magnitude of the biological pump if we are to estimate the ocean's potential for taking up and storing CO_2 from the atmosphere. Quantifying the biological pump, however, is difficult. We know that it

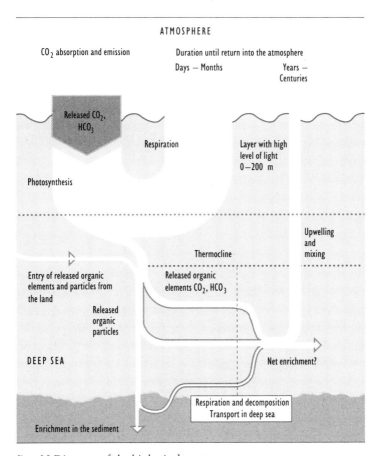

Figure 3.2 Diagram of the biological pump
Carbon related to photosynthesis sinks with dead cells to the deep ocean levels,
pumping organic material to the bottom

constitutes only a small fraction of the total amount of carbon bound via photosynthesis in a given region. What makes an assessment even more difficult is the fact that the magnitude of the pump is not constant and that instead, its magnitude depends upon the phytoplankton species present in a given region and the food chain which is supported by these phytoplankton. Why is this?

As was noted in the last chapter, the different groups of phytoplankton are, genetically speaking, less closely related to each other than the different groups of land plants. Most of the members of these different groups share the ability to bind CO_2 via photosynthesis but, in other respects, these groups can be quite different from one another.

One group, the diatoms, is characterized by the cells being encased in "shells" which contain silica – rather box-like structures with a "top" and a "bottom" lid. This cell covering makes the cells heavy compared to water. Consequently, this group of phytoplankton sinks more quickly than cells from other groups which are not encased in a heavy shell. In addition, many diatoms are large compared to the majority of phytoplankton species. Large cells sink more quickly than small cells. Thus, we can expect the biological pump to be more active (i.e. transport more carbon to the bottom waters) in a region dominated by relatively large phytoplankton cells than in a region dominated by small cells. The biological pump can be at its most effective when the large phytoplankton cells which are present are diatoms with heavy silica shells. There is, however, another reason why the biological pump can be expected to be highly active when large phytoplankton cells are present and that is the composition of the so-called grazing community, i.e. the animals that eat the phytoplankton.

Large phytoplankton cells can be eaten by large species of zooplankton, the group we refer to as "mesozooplankton" because of their size (see Figure 2.1 in Chapter 2). Copepods such as *Calanus finmarchicus* (see Plate 6 in the color section) are, for example, classified as mesozooplankton. In contrast to the smaller zooplankton ("protozooplankton") which feed on correspondingly smaller phytoplankton, copepods produce large and fairly compact faecal pellets. These pellets also sink relatively quickly to the bottom of the water column (especially when diatoms have been a part of the copepod diet and the faecal pellets contain pieces of the heavy silica shells). The presence or absence of sinking faecal pellets, therefore, represents another mechanism which can contribute to differences in the magnitude of the biological pump from region to region.

This example clearly illustrates that, in terms of the ocean's ability to retain the CO_2 which is bound through photosynthesis, the biodiversity of the phytoplankton and zooplankton communities really matters! It makes a difference which species are present, but – as we will see in Chapter 6 – there is reason to believe that changes caused by human activities can affect the composition of the species and, thereby, biodiversity in the ocean, including the biodiversity of the tiny phytoplankton and zooplankton.

The carbonate pump

The biological pump is by no means the only non-physical mechanism by which carbon can be transported from the surface to the bottom layers of the ocean. There is another method which we refer to as the "carbonate pump". With this mechanism, carbon is transported to the deeper layers of the ocean through the sinking of calcium carbonate structures (shells) created by a variety of organisms.

Why then do we differentiate between these two mechanisms, when it is biology which is ultimately responsible for both the biological and the major part of the carbonate pump? There are two reasons for this. The first is that the biological pump transports organic (living or formerly living) material to bottom waters, while calcium carbonate is not an organic substance, even though it is produced by living organisms. The other reason is that the chemistry of calcium carbonate – both with respect to its formation and its behavior in bottom waters – is quite different to that of organic material. This means that the net impact of the material transported by the two different pumps will influence the ocean's net carbon budget in different ways. However, for our purposes here it is sufficient to note that the carbonate pump is also a mechanism which can transport carbon from surface layers of the ocean to the waters near the ocean bed.

Again, it is only specific groups of organisms which contribute to the carbonate pump, i.e. those which produce calcium carbonate. Many marine organisms do this but the most important among the phytoplankton are the coccolithophorids (Fig. 3.3). Among the zooplankton, the foraminifera should be highlighted. To understand how important these two groups of tiny marine organisms are in terms of transferring carbon to the huge carbon reservoirs in the ocean sediment, we only need to consider chalk cliffs, such as the White Cliffs of Dover in the UK. These cliffs were formed via geological processes which lifted ancient sea bed to the position of the cliffs today; they consist almost entirely of the fossilized remains of coccolithophorids and foraminifera – tiny plants and animals which steadily rain down from the surface to the deeper reaches of the ocean.

The global carbon cycle and the impact of the oceans upon it are currently the focus of much scientific interest, given the unprecedented rate at which CO_2 in the Earth's atmosphere is

Figure 3.3 Electron microscope image of the coccolithophorids
Emiliania huxleyi.
The platelets (coccoliths) which cover the cell are made of calcium carbonate.
These coccoliths sink to the ocean bed and ultimately form the main component
of chalk cliffs such as those in Dover.

currently increasing and the link between global climate change
and this increased concentration of CO_2 in the atmosphere.
Accurate predictions of future climate conditions require a thorough understanding of the interactions between the oceans and
the atmosphere and, in particular, a clearer understanding of
how CO_2 is exchanged between the two. One of the reasons that
climate prediction is so difficult today is the fact that we still
know very little about the potential of the oceans to take up and
retain CO_2.

By far the most important process in terms of the uptake of atmospheric CO_2 is the physical-chemical process of balancing pressure differences. At the boundary between the atmosphere and the ocean, the CO_2 in the two media air and water is always trying to achieve equilibrium between the number of CO_2 molecules moving from the water to the air and the number of CO_2 molecules taking the opposite route. The more CO_2 there is in the atmosphere, the more dissolves in the ocean and vice versa. If there was no biological activity in the oceans, and we knew the temperature and salinity of the ocean as well as the concentration of CO_2 in the atmosphere and the rate of deep water formation (see Chapter 1), then it would be (relatively) easy to calculate the role of the oceans in absorbing atmospheric CO_2. What makes the calculation so complicated, however, is not having a full understanding of the biologically mediated processes described above. This fact should remind us that that life in the ocean (and on land) is not simply a passive passenger in an Earth System, defined by physical and chemical processes, but that it is an active participant in shaping the prevailing living conditions.

As a final note concerning the global carbon cycle, methane should also be mentioned. Most often, when we refer to the influence of greenhouse gases on climate, we use CO_2 as a proxy for all greenhouse gases. However, there are in fact a number of others which deserve more attention in terms of understanding atmosphere and climate interactions than they are receiving today. Methane is one of these gases.

Our understanding of methane production and release in and from the ocean is still very limited. It has emerged that surface waters of the ocean, which are saturated with oxygen, contain surprisingly large quantities of methane but the reasons for this are unclear. It is also known that the greatest release of methane from the ocean to the atmosphere occurs in coastal areas. We have already noted that this zone is disproportionably influenced by human activity in comparison to the rest of the ocean and, in coming chapters, we will see that chemical conditions in this zone are changing in response to this influence. Some of the changes occurring could, at least in theory, result in a greater release of methane than is the case today. Predicting the future of the oceans and their role in determining the climate of the future requires a better understanding of methane dynamics in the ocean, a field of research which is now becoming increasingly important (see Chapter 4).

Nitrogen

Another global element cycle in which the oceans and ocean biology play a major role is the nitrogen cycle (Fig. 3.4). Nitrogen (N) is a prerequisite for life as it is a building block of proteins. Seventy-eight percent of the air we breathe consists of nitrogen, so there's quite a bit of it around. However, in its gaseous form, nitrogen cannot be used directly by most living organisms. Before it can be utilized in most biological processes, nitrogen needs to be bound to hydrogen. So, although nitrogen is exceedingly abundant in our atmosphere, it is often still a limiting factor for production in biological systems. Both on land and in the ocean, there are a number of (micro) organisms which are capable of taking up nitrogen from the air and making it available for other biological systems. It should be noted here that, although we often hear about plants which are capable of nitrogen fixation, these plants which appear to bind nitrogen actually live symbiotically with micro-organisms (bacteria), the enzymes of which absorb N_2 from the atmosphere and convert it into a form which can be used by the plant.

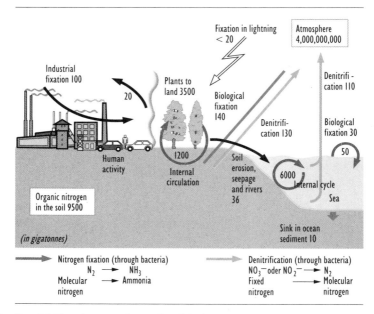

Figure 3.4 This diagram shows the global nitrogen cycle
The quantitative significance of industrial (human) activities in the transfer of
nitrogen gas from the atmosphere to the earth's production cycle is noteworthy.

Once again, we can see here that biodiversity of micro-organisms plays a vital role in ensuring that the Earth System works. Only very few micro-organisms are capable of collecting nitrogen and making it available to the rest of the biological community. In the oceans, it is believed that only cyanobacteria are capable of directly absorbing nitrogen. Until recently, the widely held belief was that nitrogen fixation in the ocean occurred only in very limited geographical regions and was only performed by a few species. However, recent developments in molecular methodology have made it possible to identify the genes which are responsible for the coding of specific proteins, and this has enabled scientists to discover that the genes involved in nitrogen fixation are more widespread in the ocean than the organisms which are known to collect nitrogen. The presence of these genes does not necessarily mean that they are active and that nitrogen fixation is actually taking place. Nevertheless, this finding suggests that nitrogen fixation may be more prevalent in the ocean than previously believed. Needless to say, the magnitude of nitrogen fixation in the ocean is still very much a subject of debate and the focus of considerable research efforts.

Nitrogen fixation involves the transfer of nitrogen from the atmosphere into the ocean; however, nitrogen can also follow this path in the opposite direction, i.e. from the ocean to the atmosphere. Gaseous nitrogen, N_2, is not only absorbed by marine organisms but is also given off by so-called denitrifying bacteria. This means that there are both ocean organisms which collect N_2 and ocean organisms which release it (once again here, biodiversity is the key). In addition, other gaseous nitrogen compounds like dinitrous oxide (N_2O) are also exchanged between the ocean and the atmosphere. Here again, though, there is no accurate quantitative information about the net exchange of these gases over the ocean-atmosphere interface.

Although it receives less attention from the general public, the global nitrogen cycle – just like the global carbon cycle – is also changing drastically in response to human activities. As explained above, in an unperturbed system, it is primarily the enzymes of a small group of microorganisms which make nitrogen available for biological production. With the invention of artificial fertilizers, humans developed the ability to chemically mimic the process carried out in nature by nitrogen-collecting microbes. Today, more nitrogen is captured from the atmosphere through human activity than by all of the biological activity of micro-organisms on land combined. This means that, since the use of artificial fertilizers has become widespread, much more nitrogen has been introduced into and is active in the biological production cycle than previously was the case. This has repercussions for the global nitrogen cycle as a whole but, also, as we will see in Chapter 5, for the biodiversity of the ocean as well as the ocean's function and role in the nitrogen cycle.

The oceans and sulfur

All living organisms need sulfur and this element is much more abundant in the ocean than on land. One of the ways in which land-based organisms obtain this vital element is through the release of sulfurous compounds from the ocean to the atmosphere (of which dimethylsulfide (DMS) is the most important). Phytoplankton are critical to a number of processes relating to the ocean's contribution to the global sulfur cycle. Firstly, they take up sulfate from seawater. Secondly, a number of phytoplankton species (but not all – here again, biodiversity of microorganisms is important) produce dimethylsulfoniumpropionate (DMSP), a precursor to DMS. The phytoplankton use DMSP for a number of metabolic processes and even as a "communication" chemical in interactions with other organisms. When the phytoplankton cell dies, DMSP is released to the surrounding water. Once in the water, it can be converted by bacteria (and even some other phytoplankton) to form different sulfur compounds which can be used metabolically. Finally, some bacteria break DMSP down to DMS, which then is released to the atmosphere.

As soon as it enters the atmosphere, DMS reacts with oxygen and small particles form on which water can accumulate. These particles are called "cloud condensation nuclei" as – in sufficient

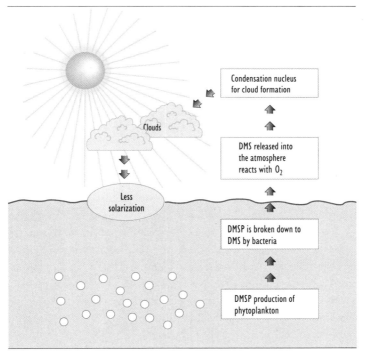

Figure 3.5 Diagram of DMS production

By releasing this compound containing sulfur, the phytoplankton has a direct influence on cloud formation and therefore climate.

quantities — the tiny water-bearing particles create clouds. It seems incredible but, in sufficient numbers, some tiny phytoplankton can actually influence the climate by creating clouds over the ocean (Fig. 3.5). These clouds alter the flow of heat in the atmosphere, so the link from these tiny organisms to our climate is complete.

In the late 1980s, a feedback loop was proposed between

phytoplankton, DMS and the climate. According to this hypothesis, a warmer and more heavily stratified ocean resulting from global warming could cause a proliferation of phytoplankton species which produce DMSP and, hence, increase DMS production. The increased DMS production could then stimulate cloud formation and thus help to cool the Earth. This "CLAW" hypothesis (whereby CLAW refers to the initials of the four authors Charlson, Lovelock, Andreae and Warren) attracted considerable interest, and DMS and its potential role in climate change has been the focus of research efforts for the last two decades. Despite this huge scientific interest, we still have no clear idea how important phytoplankton-mediated DMS production may be for climate development. There is, however, increasing evidence that climate fluctuations (for example El Niño and La Niña) do, apparently, influence biodiversity of the phytoplankton in such a manner that, under warmer and more stratified conditions, there are more species which produce DMSP and, hence, more DMS is released to the atmosphere. As a consequence, the CLAW hypothesis predicts that global warming will lead to an increase in DMS released from the ocean. It is clear that this feedback effect has not yet been able to prevent global warming (see Chapter 4) but it may have an influence on regional climate.

Accordingly, the final verdict on the possible existence of a feedback loop between phytoplankton, DMS and the climate is not yet in. Nevertheless, the fact that these so very different processes – spanning from phytoplankton metabolism to cloud formation and changes in solar radiation reaching the Earth – potentially appear to be linked, emphasizes a number of important points:

- The Earth functions as a system, in which processes occurring in the different components of the Earth System (i.e. ocean, atmosphere, and land) are interlinked.

- A change in one component in the system (i.e. the composition of the phytoplankton community) can give rise to unexpected responses in other areas of the system.
- The ocean gives us far more than just fish. It is also an important mediator in the global element cycles.
- Marine microbes play a decisive role in the global circulation of elements.
- Microbial diversity also plays a hugely important role in the Earth System performance.

Most of the organisms in the ocean are very small – so tiny, in fact, that they cannot be seen with the naked eye. Consequently, we are unable to directly appreciate the differences between them. Nonetheless, these differences are crucial in order for the oceans and the Earth System to function.

If you ask the man on the street for his views on biodiversity in the oceans and on which organisms are the most important to preserve and protect, he will, most likely, place the large animal species at the top of his list of priorities. Whales, other marine mammals and fish, along with perhaps a few bottom dwellers such as corals or starfish would probably make the list of organisms whose biodiversity should be conserved. However, in terms of the ocean and the element cycles in the Earth System, these large animals are not at all important.

When it comes to element cycles, small is beautiful and, while it is perhaps not important that all species are conserved, it is important that all microbial functions or functional groups are preserved in order for the Earth System to function. As we will see in Chapter 5, global processes are taking place which threaten to change the relative distributions of the various microbes and their functions in the ocean. If this happens, then the role of the oceans in the global element cycle may be dramatically altered.

4 Climate change and the oceans

Since the start of industrialization in the 19th century, human activities have had an increasing effect on global climate. We are right now in the middle of a period of climate change which also has many different effects on the world's oceans. In this chapter, we will first take a look at physical changes such as increases in water temperatures and rising sea levels. Chapters 5 and 6 will then discuss the chemical and biological changes occurring in the oceans, some of which are linked to climate change and some of which are caused by other human activities.

The greenhouse effect and global warming

During the past 150 years, the concentration of carbon dioxide in the Earth's atmosphere has risen by a third from 280 ppm (parts per million) to the current level of 385 ppm (2008). This marks the highest CO_2 concentration for at least 650,000 years (this is how far back scientists have been able to obtain accurate CO_2 data for the atmosphere from ice cores) but it is probably the highest concentration for millions of years. This rise has entirely been caused by human activity: the additional 100 ppm actually only corresponds to about half of the quantity we have emitted. If it were not for the fact that the oceans and forests have taken up some of our emissions from the atmosphere, then we would have already caused almost twice the current increase in atmospheric concentration. (In a later chapter, we will discuss whether the ocean and land biospheres will continue to be able to absorb a similar proportion of our emissions or whether this portion may diminish, thereby further aggravating the climate problem.)

The concentrations of a number of other gases in the atmosphere have also been drastically changed as a result of human activities. Methane concentration has more than doubled, while levels of nitrogen oxide have risen by one fifth. Some other gases we find today do not naturally occur in the atmosphere at all and have only accumulated there through human intervention, i.e. the chlorofluorocarbons (CFCs). Although the production of CFCs has now been banned internationally through the Montreal Protocol in recognition of their destructive effects on the stratospheric ozone layer, these gases will dwell in the atmosphere for decades to come, damaging the ozone layer and influencing climate patterns in the process.

All of these gases share one important property: they act as greenhouse gases, which means that they alter the radiation balance of Earth. They absorb a portion of the thermal energy radiated by the Earth's surface and our atmosphere, thereby interfering with the emission of heat into space. This so-called "greenhouse effect" is a physical phenomenon which has been known since the 19th century.

A climate equilibrium is established when the amount of heat emitted from Earth exactly matches the amount of incident solar energy. If this emission of heat radiation is blocked, then the climate goes out of equilibrium, with more heat being absorbed than emitted and this, of course, causes temperatures to rise. As a consequence of this warming, emission of radiated heat also increases – so, at a higher concentration of greenhouse gases, a

new equilibrium can be subsequently established at a higher temperature level. However, as was already touched on in Chapter
1, there will be a delay period before the new equilibrium is
reached, as the oceans require a relatively long period of time to
warm up to a new temperature level.

The climatic effects of individual greenhouse gases are measured in terms of their quantitative effect on the radiation balance
– and this is measured in Watts, i.e. the same units used for light
bulbs or heaters, although in terms of greenhouse gasses, the
measurement is given for one square meter of the Earth's surface.
Accordingly, the increase in CO_2 concentration to date has had
a heating effect (the technical term is "radiative forcing") of
1.7 W/m² (Watts per square meter). The increase in methane concentration is responsible for a further 0.5 W/m² and the CFC
increase for at least 0.3 W/m²; the increased concentration of
ground level ozone (not to be confused with the loss of stratospheric ozone) produces a further 0.3 W/m² and nitrogen oxide
nearly 0.2 W/m². Together, these greenhouse gases, thus, contribute an additional greenhouse effect of 3 W/m². (The word
"additional" is used here because, of course, there is also an
abundance of natural greenhouse gases that are responsible for
the natural greenhouse effect, without which the Earth would be
completely frozen and hostile.)

In addition to these greenhouse gases, human activities have
another important influence on the climate: the pollution of the
atmosphere with particles (dust, soot, sulfur particles etc.); these
aerosols are also commonly referred to as smog. As these particles reflect sunlight, they have a cooling effect on the climate.
Quantifying this effect is significantly more difficult than quantifying the effects of greenhouse gases – and, although its value
is estimated at 1.2 W/m², the associated uncertainty is higher.
This means that around one-third of the additional greenhouse

effect is compensated for by particles released to the atmosphere – but only if global averages are considered. In contrast to greenhouse gases, which as a result of their longevity are well mixed throughout the entire atmosphere, occurrences of smog – and, therefore, the radiation-related effects on climate – vary greatly from one region to another.

A third human influence on climate is through a change in brightness of land areas (the so-called albedo) arising from changes in land use, for example as a result of deforestation and subsequent conversion of land for agricultural use. This has a cooling effect of around 0.2 W/m². Taking all of these factors into account, the effects of human activities are responsible for a net increase of 1.6 W/m² in the radiation balance.

So what are the consequences of this change in the radiation balance? As explained above, the resulting imbalance will invariably lead to a warming of the global climate but how much warmer will it get? Calculating the exact extent of this warming is by no means easy, as it depends upon a number of feedback effects which can amplify or weaken the warming. These include changes in the water vapor concentration in the atmosphere; water vapor is the most important greenhouse gas in the atmosphere and its concentration increases with rising temperatures. This will amplify any warming (or cooling). They also include changes in the cloud cover – different types of clouds at different altitudes can both weaken or boost warming effects. Finally, they also include changes in the snow and ice cover on our planet. As bright ice surfaces reflect a great deal of solar radiation, any loss of ice cover means an increased absorption of solar heat; this boosts the warming, particularly at higher latitudes. In Chapter 1, it was explained how the world's oceans play a decisive role in all three of these feedback loops, one of the reasons being the fact that evaporation from the enormous, open bodies of water comprising the world's oceans represents the primary source of atmospheric water vapor and, hence, cloud water, as well as the primary source of snow and ice. A "dry" planet without large oceans would react completely differently to increases in atmospheric CO_2 concentration than our ocean planet.

The net effect of all of these feedback loops is to amplify the effects of climate change. This is the clear conclusion drawn from all model calculations. This is also the conclusion supported by historical evidence, which shows that dramatic climate changes have taken place repeatedly throughout the history of the Earth (one example being the well-known ice ages). If the feedback in the Earth's climate system would have tended to have an overall weakening effect rather than a strengthening one, then the natural climate fluctuations occurring in the past would have been much weaker and less spectacular.

Climatologists use the so-called "climate sensitivity" as a measure of the sensitivity of the climate system to disturbances. This parameter indicates the degree to which the equilibrium temperature of the Earth (by which we always mean the globally averaged air temperature close to the surface) changes in response to a particular change in the radiation balance. Accordingly, it is measured in degrees Celsius per Watt per square meter and it can be used to calculate the number of degrees by which the climate will heat up, for example as a result of the 1.6 W/m² increase introduced by humans into the system. Another indicator which is even simpler and more widespread is the expected rise in temperature if the CO_2 concentration is doubled (which corresponds to a change of the radiation balance by 3.7 W/m²). According to current understanding, this climate sensitivity is around 3 °C, with an uncertainty of around ±1 °C. The uncertainty is due to the fact that we can only determine the magnitude of the feedbacks described above within certain uncertainty margins; no serious scientist would quote this type of value without indicating the potential error (or uncertainty) associated with it. 3 °C for a doubling of the CO_2 concentration – i.e. 3.7 W/m^2 – corresponds to 0.8 °C per W/m^2 perturbation of the radiation balance.

In media reports, the climate sensitivity is constantly confused with the temperature increase predicted by the year 2100 because the numbers are similar for scenarios in which no efforts are made to protect the climate. This is because while the CO_2 concentration could more than double (if not triple) by the year 2100, the climate system lags behind in its response because – as was already explained – the oceans are slow to change their temperature. As a result, the level of warming is initially less than that which will be achieved when equilibrium is reached. This could lead us to a level of warming by 2100 that is quite similar to the magnitude of the climate sensitivity. There is, however, a very important point here: the level of warming by 2100 depends on us, i.e. on our emissions. If we take decisive action to protect the climate, then the level of warming by 2100 could be significantly less than 2 °C. By contrast, if we allow very high emissions of CO_2 into the atmosphere then the climate could be warmed by 6 °C or even more. We have no influence at all on the climate sensitivity – and this makes it a particularly useful parameter for climate research, as it is a purely physical property of the climate system that does not depend on human activities.

The actual warming at a given time is thus a product of the perturbation of the radiation balance multiplied by the climate sensitivity, corrected by a percentage factor which expresses the thermal "sluggishness" or inertia of the climate system, i.e. the extent to which the changes we can observe lag behind the changes occurring in the underlying climate system. So, taking all of this into account, how much global warming has been caused by humans? As discussed above, the perturbation of the radiation balance caused by humans to date is around 1.6 W/m² – which corresponds to 3 W/m² due to greenhouse gas emissions minus approximately 1.4 W/m² due to the aerosol pollution and changes in the brightness of the Earth's land surface. Applying the best estimate climate sensitivity value described above of 0.8 °C per W/m², we obtain a warming, at equilibrium, of 0.8 × 1.6 = 1.3 °C. Due to the thermal lag of the climate system, only half to two-thirds of this warming can be predicted to have taken place so far. In total, this produces a theoretical prediction of global warming caused by humans of 0.7 to 0.9 °C to date. This prediction agrees well with temperature measurements which indicate that a global warming of 0.8 °C has taken place since the start of industrialization.

Incidentally, measurements have also shown that the known natural causes of changes in the radiation balance, which have repeatedly led to climate fluctuations throughout history, can be excluded in the case of the temperature increase recorded since the onset of industrialization. There has been no increase in solar activity in the last 60 years and the orbital parameters of the Earth (which previously triggered the ice ages) also offer no explanation for present warming.

From the above, it can be concluded that a further increase in the concentration of greenhouse gases will further drive global temperatures up. How far up depends largely on us: specifically, it depends upon how much carbon dioxide and other greenhouse gases are emitted into the atmosphere by humans during the next decades. Climatologists are unable to predict this – we can only calculate the expected level of warming that will be triggered if a particular quantity of greenhouse gases is emitted (a so-called "emissions scenario"). These scenarios are published by the Intergovernmental Panel on Climate Change (IPCC) at regular intervals. The task of the IPCC is to assess the latest scientific understanding of climate change, as it is documented in thousands of scientific journals. Hundreds of climatologists engage in intensive discussions in order to write the IPCC reports, which are then assessed in a wide-ranging, three-stage review process. According to the most recent report published in 2007 and depending on the emissions scenario, a further increase in the average global temperature of between 1 and 6 °C is to be expected by the year 2100. During the next few decades, regardless of scenario, the temperature will probably rise by 0.2 °C per decade, a figure which corresponds approximately to the rate of increase seen over the last three decades. Taking into account the fact that emissions are not going to change abruptly, atmospheric CO_2 has a cumulative effect and the climate system has an inertia as explained above (see Chapter 1), different emission scenarios will only lead to differences in temperature increases later on, with clear differences only becoming obvious from the middle of the century and thereafter.

Warming of the oceans

In 2006, newspapers reported record high temperatures in the North Sea. During the month of October, the average water temperature was warmer than ever before – at least since measurements began – and, at 14.2 °C, it was more than 2.4 °C above the long-term average from 1968 to 1993. The German Federal Maritime and Hydrographic Agency interpreted this as an "unmistakable sign of the start of climate change in the North Sea."

This snapshot of the sea at the heart of Northern Europe from October 2006 is just one piece in a much bigger and more comprehensive picture: the long-term global increase in water temperatures in the oceans. Fig. 4.1 shows how temperatures have developed during the period from 1860 to 2000. During this period, the sea surface temperatures have increased on average by 0.6 °C – i.e. slightly less than the globally averaged air temperature. Their development has followed a similar path to that of air temperature: an initial period of warming at the start of the 20th century was followed by a period of stagnation from around 1940 to 1980 and a further period of warming in the period since. This variation over time can be explained by the fact that, during the initial warming phase (up to 1940), increasing solar activity and the increasing concentration of greenhouse gases combined to heat up the climate. From 1940 onwards, the continued increase in greenhouse gases was offset by the rise in cooling aerosol pollution (smog), while solar activity remained more or less constant. In the 1970s, further increase in aerosol pollution was stopped because of its harmful effects on health. The solar activity during this period remained virtually unchanged (if anything, it displayed a slight downward trend over the past 20 years) and, as a result, the ever accelerating rise in greenhouse gas concentration has become the dominant influence on climate.

However, if we only look at global averages, this will disguise the fact that there are – in some cases – substantial regional variations in ocean temperatures and the patterns in their development. There are two reasons for this: firstly, the climate system on Earth has always been characterized by natural fluctuations with many different causes and these fluctuations are superimposed on the long-term global trends. When viewed as a global average over a period of several years, these fluctuations are relatively small, but – as can be seen in Fig. 4.1 – the smaller the size of the region and period under investigation, the larger the magnitude of these fluctuations can be. In addition, man-made

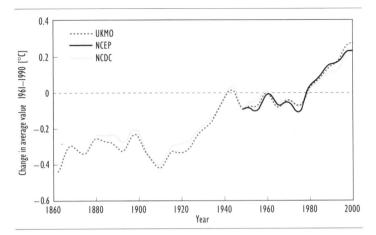

Figure 4.1 Increase in the surface temperature of the oceans (global average) according to three different data centers

climate change can have different impacts in different regions. For example, the increase in water temperatures is particularly pronounced in areas where global warming causes shrinkage of the ocean's ice cover. This, in turn, leads to further warming due to the ice-albedo feedback effect. In fact, some parts of the Arctic Ocean have seen an increase in temperature of more than 3 °C in recent decades, which is several times higher than the global trend for the same period. At the same time, the size of the ice cover in the Arctic Sea is shrinking more and more – with almost half now having been lost since satellite observations began in 1979. A new study published in 2006 came to the conclusion that the Arctic Sea could be ice-free during the summer months as soon as 2040. Previous model calculations had predicted that this would not happen until the last quarter of the century. A record low was reached in 2007: with 4 million square kilometers, the ice cover was only half the size it had still been during the 1960s.

In contrast, changes to currents and winds in some regions can even result in cooling – caused, paradoxically, by global warming. For example, one region of sea to the south of Greenland has displayed a noticeable cooling throughout the past century – a development which counters the otherwise universal trend toward warmer temperatures. A cooling in this region has also been predicted by many simulation models as a consequence of the weakening of the North Atlantic Current (see also the section entitled "Changes to the Ocean Currents" below). Careful analyses with a combination of simulation models and data measurements are required in order to clarify whether the former (superimposed natural fluctuations) or the latter (a regional, man-made effect) is responsible for the temperature changes noted in each case.

So far, we have only looked at temperature changes close to the surface of the ocean. This layer of water is in direct contact with the atmosphere and is, therefore, directly affected by changes in the radiation balance. As was explained in Chapter 1, this uppermost, well-mixed layer of the ocean has a depth of approximately 50 to 200 meters depending on latitude. Now it is time to turn our attention to the ocean underneath. How can we expect this part of the ocean to respond to climate change?

In the long term, it can be predicted that the increase in temperature – which only affects the surface initially – will gradually spread to deeper ocean layers; in most regions through slow mixing processes but more quickly in areas where volumes of water sink down from the surface to greater depths. However, it is difficult to predict the rate at which this penetration will take place, as it depends on both the regional temperature changes – particularly in the deep water formation areas – and on possible changes in the deep water formation process itself.

It is possible to measure the gradual warming of the deeper water layers – even though the data coverage here leaves a lot to be desired, as the temperatures at depth in the oceans have only been measured from research and expedition ships in the past. It is only in recent years that larger numbers of autonomous probes, the so-called Argo floats, have been used. These cylinders measure approximately two meters in height, are equipped with a battery of measuring instruments, drift at a depth of 2000 meters and surface every ten days. Among other data, they record temperature profiles and subsequently transmit the data to satellites. Around 3000 of these floats (each costing approximately € 25,000) are currently deployed and active in the world's oceans, where they form a network which offers a previously unattainable density of temperature data. The available data show that a warming of 0.1 °C or more during the last fifty years is still restricted to the upper 500 meters in most of the oceans. Only in a few areas has the warming penetrated to depths greater than 1000 meters and beyond – most notably, the North Atlantic between 20 and 40 degrees latitude north. However, if we go even further north in the Atlantic, i.e., between 50 and 60 degrees latitude north, a cooling of temperatures is measured down to very great depths. It is thought that this is a consequence of the already-mentioned cooling which is taking place at the surface in this region; the knock-on cooling effect is the result of dense cold water sinking down to great depths.

The total amount of heat absorbed by the ocean is of particular interest (see Fig. 4.2). Changes in the heat content of the world's oceans can be calculated from the global ocean temperatures. During the past 40 years (from 1961 to 2003 to be precise), the ocean has gained 1.4×10^{23} J of energy. This corresponds to 400 times the current level of global energy production – but, despite this, ocean temperatures have only increased by less than

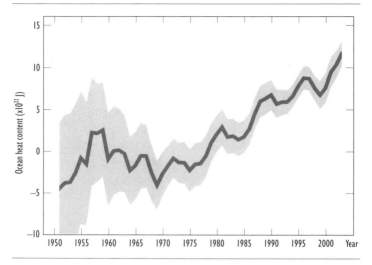

Figure 4.2 Change in the heat content of the world's oceans (up to a
depth of 700 meters) since 1950
There is a clear increase over the long-term despite short-term variations

0.04 °C on average (in relation to the total volume of ocean
water).

If we convert the heat absorption of the ocean into a number
of Watts per square meter of the Earth's surface, then it is
possible to directly compare the absorption to the greenhouse
gas heating effect explained above – this value is presently
1.6 W/m² (including an allowance for the cooling effects of smog).
During the period from 1961 to 2003, the oceans absorbed heat
at an average rate of 0.4 W/m². This shows that a significant
portion of the additional thermal radiation caused by anthro-
pomorphic greenhouse gases "disappears" in the oceans – and
this is, itself, an expression of the buffering effect of the oceans

on the global climate, i.e. the thermal "sluggishness" already described above.

It is worth noting that the oceans are the only part of the climate system that can take up so much heat. The combined storage of heat in the atmosphere and the land masses only amounts to around 10% of that of the oceans. Furthermore, the total energy consumed globally for the melting of ice (i.e. melting glaciers and shrinking polar sea ice cover and ice sheets) is negligible by comparison. This may come as a surprise to some but it is linked to the poor thermal conductivity of ice. It does, however, also show that, in terms of energy, it would be no problem for the global ice masses to melt much more quickly if only they were in closer contact with the heat. This is not a completely absurd thought, as these ice masses are becoming increasingly wet – meltwater penetrates into glacier cracks and crevasses, streams of ice flow increasingly quickly towards the sea, where they then come into contact with warmer ocean water. As anyone who has ever defrosted a freezer will know, ice melts very slowly even under warm summer temperatures – but it melts a lot faster if it is placed in a bucket of water.

Rising sea levels

The previous paragraphs have led directly to the subject of rising sea levels – and both of the main causes of sea level rise have already been mentioned: melting land ice adds water to the sea and increasing water temperatures cause ocean water to expand. The satellites Topex/Poseidon and Jason have been mapping the surface height of the Earth's oceans with great accuracy since 1993. Data obtained with the aid of these satellites have shown a global rise in sea levels by 3.3 mm per year. However, what we

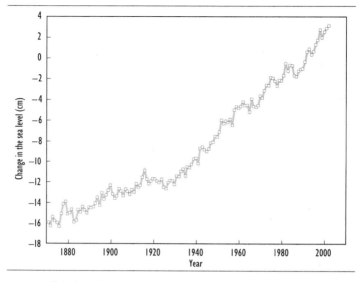

Figure 4.3 Global sea level rise as measured by tide gauges at the coasts

The curve shows real changes in the volume of ocean water, i.e. the effect of rising and sinking land in response to the end of the last Ice Age has already been accounted for

really want to know is this: when did sea levels start to rise and by how much has the surface of the oceans approximately risen during the last century?

Data from sea level measurements at numerous coastal towns all around the world are available for the period before satellite measurements began. However, coastal data have three disadvantages: firstly, they offer no information away from the coasts; secondly, the accuracy and homogeneity of the data records is often questionable; and finally, sea levels close to coastal areas may be influenced by rising or sinking land mass, which needs to be corrected for with great care.

Accordingly, the best currently available sea level curve for the period since 1880 combines particularly reliable measurements of coastal sea levels with the satellite data. The two are intercalibrated for the period in which both sets of data overlap. According to this curve, the sea level has risen by 18 cm since 1880, as can be seen in Figure 4.3. This is a new phenomenon: there has been no – even vaguely – comparable rise in the past millennia. This is known among other things from analyses of structures like sea walls dating back to Roman times, which are known to have been constructed at a particular height in relation to the sea level. Furthermore, if levels had been rising at a rate of 18 cm per century then, even as recently as the Middle Ages, levels would have to have been about two meters lower than they are now, which was clearly not the case. As the current rise in sea levels is, for all practical purposes, an entirely modern phenomenon, we have to assume that it has been caused by the most recent global warming.

In principle, three factors can change global sea levels: firstly, the addition of more water; secondly, a change in density of the water (thermal expansion); and, thirdly, a geological change in the volume of the ocean basins. The latter plays an important role over the course of hundreds of millions of years but is less important in terms of current trends: as a long-term consequence of the last ice age and the disappearance of the enormous continental ice masses at the end of the ice age (around 10,000 years ago), the ocean basins are increasing slightly in size, which in itself would have caused sea levels to drop by 0.3 mm per year – so this effect slightly counters the rise measured above.

Thermal expansion in turn is a straightforward consequence of warming – warmer water occupies a larger volume than colder water. Roughly speaking, the resulting rise in the sea level is proportional to the increased heat content of the oceans which has already been discussed above. However, if we look at this a little more closely, we see that this is, in fact, not the case, as thermal expansion varies greatly as a function of temperature and salinity. This means that expansion is not just a matter of the total amount of heat absorbed by the ocean; it also matters *where* this heat is absorbed. If sea water is heated by one degree from 20 °C to 21 °C, its volume will increase by more than four times as much as if it is heated from 0 °C to 1 °C. So, for sea level, it really matters whether the temperature changes most in tropical seas or the polar oceans.

For the period from 1961 to 2003, the warming of ocean waters already described has led to a rise in sea levels of 0.4 mm per year due to thermal expansion – this can be calculated on the basis of the temperature measurements. In addition there is an estimated contribution of 0.5 mm per year from shrinking mountain glaciers and 0.2 mm per year from melting large continental ice masses in Greenland and Antarctica. These contributions add up to a total of 1.1 mm per year. However, the actual increase measured is 1.8 mm per year. Rather than being the result of some major "forgotten" contributing factor which affects sea levels, this discrepancy is most probably attributable to the significant uncertainties attached to all of these numbers – the difference is just within overall uncertainty. For the last decade (1993 to 2003), the numbers are more reliable and closer together: the individual components add up to a total of 2.8 mm per year, while the measured rise in sea levels is 3.1 mm per year. In the current decade, the continental ice masses (equal parts Greenland and Antarctica) contribute 0.4 mm, mountain glaciers 0.8 mm and thermal expansion 1.6 mm per year. These more recent data, therefore, offer a consistent picture, albeit one lacking the desired level of accuracy.

The situation is more difficult for the model calculations

which are being used to project future sea levels. These models are usually started in the 18th century – i.e. before the start of any discernable human impact on climate – and then calculate global climate progression on the basis of the increasing concentration of greenhouse gases and other driving factors (aerosols pollutions, solar activity, and volcanic activity) and the laws of physics. The temperature curves calculated with the aid of these models do a good job of matching historical data measurements, so the temperatures forecast with their aid for the future are regarded as being quite reliable. However, these models underestimate the amount by which the sea levels have risen so far. For the period of 1961 to 2003, they only yield an average rise of 5 cm, whereas the actual measured rise is 7.5 cm, i.e. 50% more. In addition, the contributions of the continental ice masses have been added here from the measured data, as the climate models are not yet able to calculate changes in the continental ice reliably. These facts – in particular, our present inability to make reliable predictions about the rate at which the continental ice masses are shrinking – mean that predictions of future changes in sea level are much less reliable than predictions of changes in temperature.

Depending on the chosen scenario and model, the model projections discussed above forecast a rise in sea level of between 18 and 59 cm by the year 2100. However, as a result of the inaccuracies already identified, the rise of the seas may turn out to be far greater than this. On the basis of data measured during the 20th century, it has been shown that the more quickly temperatures rise, the faster sea levels increase. There is a highly significant correlation between the rate at which the sea levels rise and the degree of warming observed; according to this, the sea level rises by around 3.4 mm per year for every degree of warming (this means that a warming of 0.5° C results in a rise of 1.7 mm per

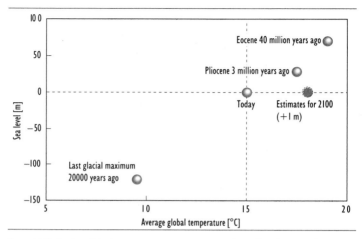

Figure 4.4 Relationship between temperature and sea level in earth's recent history

The diagram shows the changes in sea level (compared to today) at different climatic periods with colder and warmer climates. The rise in the sea level projected until 2100 is negligible in comparison with the examples from earth's history as it is anticipated to be only the beginning of a much greater long-term increase.

year etc.). If we assume that this correlation will also remain effective in future, this would produce a far greater rise in sea levels – possibly even more than one meter by the year 2100 if global warming is very high and exceeds 4 °C. Whether or not this will happen is impossible to predict but the result illustrates the tremendous degree of uncertainty with regard to the prediction of future sea levels. Even if the rate at which the sea levels rise does not increase any further from now on, but instead – despite increasing temperatures – remains at the currently measured rate of 3.1 mm per year, then the height of the oceans would still increase by 31 cm within this century.

Another key point here is, again, the fact that the rise in sea levels will not stop in the year 2100, even if we have been able to stop the global warming induced by human activities by then (which we hope). Sea levels react only very slowly and with a time lag. It takes many centuries for the warming at the surface to penetrate down into the deep ocean; furthermore, it also takes many centuries or even millennia for large continental ice masses to melt. Consequently, whatever the forecasts are for the year 2100 – whether only 30 cm or more than one meter – this only marks the start of a long-lasting rise which will run the course of many centuries.

The history of climate on Earth offers clear indicators and a stark warning of the rise in sea levels we can expect in the long term. Throughout the Earth's history, global climate changes have always gone hand-in-hand with large changes in sea levels. For example, during the last ice age, the global average temperature was only around 5 °C colder than today, yet the surface of the oceans was 120 meters lower, and the islands which make up the British Isles today were part of the European continent. Another example is from the Pliocene epoch around three million years ago. This was the last time it was significantly warmer than it is now – by 2 to 3 °C on global average – and sea levels were 25 to 35 meters higher than they are now (see Fig. 4.4). The reason for this was big changes in the continental ice masses. Even today, there is still enough continental ice on Earth to raise sea levels worldwide by around 70 meters. This recently led US climatologist James Hansen, who is the head of NASA's climate institute, to describe these ice masses as a "ticking time bomb."

The fact is that, in recent years, both ice masses – in Greenland and Antarctica – have displayed increasing signs of decay around their edges. The size of the area visible from satellites in which the ice has melted in Greenland increased by around

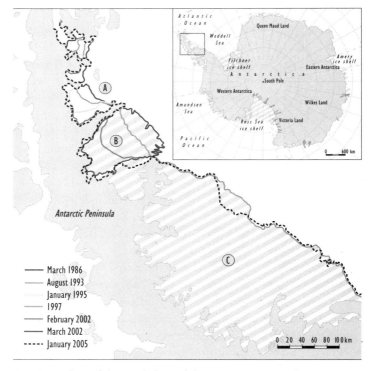

Figure 4.5 Decline of the ice shelves of the Antarctic Peninsula since 1986
The lines show the ice boundaries in different years.

25% between 1979 and 2005 and large flows of meltwater have
formed in some areas. In Greenland, around half of the ice
flows out through a dozen large outlet glaciers towards the sea;
many of these glaciers (including the Jakobshavn Isbrae) have
now doubled their flow rate. On the Antarctic Peninsula, the ice
shelves are gradually breaking up (these are glacier tongues which
have flowed out onto the ocean). The collapse of the millennia-

old Larsen B ice shelf in February 2002 was particularly spectacular. Although the disappearance of the shelf ice has no direct influence on sea levels because this ice is already floating on the sea, recent data have shown that, after the collapse of the shelf ice, the glaciers behind this ice flow more quickly towards the sea – and this transports new ice into the ocean, where it helps to raise the sea level. It is difficult to measure the mass balance of the continental ice sheets, so there is still much uncertainty over the numbers. Nonetheless, different measurements have shown that both ice sheets have lost mass during the last ten years. The hope expressed in 2001 in the 3rd IPCC report that the Antarctic ice mass might increase as a result of additional snowfall caused by climate warming and potentially, thereby, act as a brake on rising sea levels, has unfortunately not been fulfilled to date.

Different consequences in different regions

What will the consequences of rising sea levels be? In considering this question, it is important to recognize that the amount by which sea levels rise will vary substantially between different regions – so far we have only been discussing the global average. However, the surface of the oceans is not flat, but instead has hills and valleys. Due to the Earth's rotation, the surface of the ocean is inclined at right angles to currents – for example, the water on the right-hand side of the Gulf Stream is around one meter higher than it is on the left-hand side. Any change in ocean currents, therefore, causes regional changes in sea levels; however, as the water is merely re-distributed, these changes balance each other out in the global mean. Consequently, the sea level changes measured by satellites show regions where the surface has risen much faster than average (for example in Indonesia and New

Zealand), alongside regions in which sea levels have dropped
during the last decade (for example, in large parts of the Indian
Ocean). Normally, however, this type of regional variability is
generally limited to a few tens of centimeters (one exception to
this being the potential shutdown of the North Atlantic Current,
which is discussed below). This means that the global rise will
prevail everywhere in the long term, outweighing regional fluctuations in sea levels in the process. However, an additional rise
of even 10 to 15 centimeters – which is forecast according to the
simulation calculations of the latest IPCC report for the North
Sea region by the year 2100 – will significantly worsen the sea
level problem.

Another regional effect is the gravitational pull of the big ice
sheets, which weakens when these ice sheets shrink. Paradoxically, melting of Greenland ice is expected to cause a *drop* in sea
level along the coast of Greenland, because less ice there means
that less water is pulled towards Greenland. The far-field effects
of this, for example at the European coasts, are still poorly
understood, but may be substantial.

In addition, the height of land masses also changes as a result
of geological processes, particular in latitudes which bore the
weight of heavy continental ice masses during the last ice age.
A good example of this is Scotland, where the weight of the ice
masses pressing down on the land caused the land mass of the
British Isles to tilt slightly. Scotland has been rising again since the
ice masses melted around 10,000 years ago and this weight was
taken off, while southern parts of England – including London
– have been gradually sinking. At the most northerly point of
the Baltic Sea, the center of the Fennoscandic ice mass, the land
is still rising at a rate of up to 9 mm per year – i.e. three times
the rate at which global sea levels are rising. By contrast, further
south at the German coast of the Baltic, the land is sinking by

around 1 mm per year, which worsens the problems associated with changing sea levels.

Along the German coast in the North Sea, the average relative rise in sea level has been around 2 mm per year for the last few millennia, mostly due to the sinking of land in the post-ice age period. Although this is a slow and steady process, the problems associated with it have come to light episodically during dramatic storm surges. Examples include the St. Juliana flood of 1164, the St. Marcellus flood of 1219 (approximate death toll 10,000), St. Lucius' flood of 1287 (around 50,000 deaths) and the "*Grote Mandrenke*" which occurred on January 16, 1362 (approximately 100,000 deaths), during which the fabled town of Rungholt vanished in the floods. The erosion due to these and other storm surges caused the collapses of Dollart and Jadebusen, along with the formation of the Halligen islands in northern Germany as the remains of a large North Frisian land mass. This threat to land and life was countered by the local population with increasing success as dyke systems were improved hand-in-hand with technological advances and a higher degree of social organization. The construction of dykes was seen as a communal responsibility and everybody had to make a contribution – to the point where freeloaders could have their land seized if they failed to pull their weight. The last severe storm surge disasters occurred in 1953 (North Sea flood with around 1300 fatalities in the Netherlands) and 1962 (another North Sea flood, this time resulting in around 300 deaths in Hamburg); however, there was no significant loss of land on either occasion.

If we add the expected rise of 10 to 15 cm along Germany's coasts as a result of changes to sea currents to the 10 to 20 cm that the land mass is expected to sink by the year 2100, then a combined relative rise of the sea level in relation to the land of 20 to 35 cm above the mean global rise can be expected in Germany;

Figure 4.6 The German North Sea coast with the Alt-Nordstrand island
on a map by Johannes Blaeu, 1662
Only the Halligen islands remain today of the area that was once land.

accordingly, if the global rise is for example 50 cm, this could mean a rise of 70 to 85 cm in Germany. These numbers have an additional uncertainty due to the far-field gravity effects of the shrinking ice masses in Greenland and Antarctica, which cannot yet be predicted with confidence.

In addition to the natural processes of sinking and rising land masses, there is another problem which aggravates the situation concerning sea level rise: localized sinking of land as a result of human intervention. Many large towns and cities have evolved in river mouths, where they have been built on relatively soft subsoil. As a result of the weight of the buildings and the removal of groundwater, many of these cities are sinking, including Tianjin, Shanghai, Osaka, Tokyo, Bangkok, Manila, Jakarta and parts of Los Angeles. The main reason that New Orleans sustained such severe damage in 2005 as a result of the flooding caused by Hurricane Katrina was that parts of the city had sunk up to 3 meters below sea level. The protection offered by dykes was not enough. Another well-known example is the city of Venice, were the famous Piazza San Marco is flooded with an increasing frequency due to the combination of sinking land and the modern rise in sea levels (it is now flooded up to 100 times per year). In 2003 Prime Minister Berlusconi launched an ambitious storm surge defense system under the name of MOSE (*Modulo Sperimentale Elettromeccanico*, or Experimental Electromechanical Module in English), a play on the Italian name for Moses, which isolates the entire Venetian Lagoon from the Adriatic Sea in the event of a high flood.

For all of these reasons, the consequences of future rises in sea levels will vary greatly from one region to another. Initially, their impact will be felt wherever coastal cities are already under threat from sinking land; here, the rising sea levels will, thus, intensify an already existing and difficult problem. This is the case, for example, for London, where the Thames Barrier now needs to be closed more than ten times a year. This is in a marked contrast to the 1980s, when this only happened approximately once a year. In some other regions, the tectonic lifting of land masses, a repercussion from the last ice age, will compensate for any rises in sea level for at least another 100 years.

As these examples suggest, the problems associated with rising sea levels will become particularly apparent during storm surges. On a calm day, a sea level increase of even one meter would hardly be a serious problem for most coastal regions in the world. However, the disaster waiting to happen creeps up over a period of decades – only to suddenly make itself apparent during a period of just a few hours on a single day. A total of fifteen of the world's twenty megacities (defined as cities with more than 10 million inhabitants) are situated by the sea; in addition, there are also sensitive infrastructure facilities, for example nuclear power stations, which use sea water for cooling purposes. Research has been carried out on New York, for example, by the climate research institute of NASA which is based in the heart of Manhattan. Their conclusions are unsettling: a storm surge with water levels around 3 meters above normal, which today is a once-a-century event (so, statistically speaking, occurs once every 100 years), could be expected to occur every three or four years if present sea water levels were to rise by one meter. A less severe storm surge, which occurred in December 1992 (approximately 2.5 meters above normal levels), already caused massive damage, disrupting the subway system, flooding the Battery Park Tunnel, and resulting in the closure of La Guardia airport and many vital road connections. The more sea levels rise, the weaker storms need to be in order to cause this level of flooding. After a rise of 1 meter, floods like the one in December 1992 would occur on almost an annual basis. Plans are being discussed in New York for a system with three mobile storm surge barriers, which would at least protect Manhattan and, therefore, limit the extent of damage resulting from storm surges.

The consequences of rising sea levels are, of course, not restricted to the prominent coastal cities mentioned above and, in many places, complex and expensive coastal protection structures under discussion for New York are either unafford-able or completely impractical. We mentioned in Chapter 1 that the length of the world's coastlines is estimated at around one million kilometers. Only a vanishingly small proportion of this coastline can be protected and then only to a certain degree. If water levels rise even further – by 3, 4 or even 5 meters in centuries to come – then even the most expensive flood barriers and dykes will be completely useless and we will have to give up some of our cities. It is at least questionable whether this would happen in a planned and organized fashion before a storm flood disaster happens – or whether people would give up their cities only after disaster has struck.

Low-lying atolls are at particular risk, such as the Maldives and Marshall Islands, Kiribati, Tuvalu and Tokelau. Together, these island states are home to over 500,000 people but, on average, they lie just 2 meters above sea level and could become uninhabitable or even disappear altogether as a result of climate change.

On the coral atoll of Vanuatu, it has already been necessary to relocate the town of Lateu to higher ground. In the island state of Tuvalu, villagers now regularly find themselves knee-deep in water at spring tide in the village square. Many inhabitants have already emigrated to New Zealand. Alongside the numerous people who are still homeless and have not been able to return to New Orleans since Hurricane Katrina struck, these people are among the first "ocean refugees" of the 21st century. The government of New Zealand has already signed agreements with several island states about accepting these ocean refugees. It is foreseeable that a number of small island states will sink before the end of this century.

Other areas which are at particular risk include low-lying river delta regions, which offer very fertile soil and are, hence, often densely populated. One example of this is the enormous Ganges-Brahmaputra-Meghna river delta in the Gulf of Bengal, which extends from India through Bangladesh and Nepal as far as China and Bhutan. In the past, storm surges here have caused natural disasters and hundreds of thousands of deaths. The risk increases steadily together with the sea levels; however, it can – and should – be at least reduced with the aid of further local precautionary measures. In December 2006, Indian newspapers reported the disappearance of two islands in the Sundarbans, a mangrove ecosystem in the Ganges delta, a region in which tigers still roam through the forests. The flooding of the islands of Suparibhanga and Lohacharra left 10,000 people homeless; another 100,000 will need to be evacuated in the next decades.

Rising sea levels also cause increased coastal erosion and result in the loss of sandy beaches, where the processes which replenish sediment cannot keep up with the rising levels. On the German island of Sylt in the North Sea, sand is already being replenished artificially in order to fight the loss of sand on the island's beaches; this measure makes good commercial sense due to the high volume of income generated by tourism here. This practice is also widespread in Spanish holiday resorts, where beaches are currently being regenerated in 400 different locations. Along many other coasts, beaches are becoming smaller or disappearing altogether as a result of the rise in sea levels.

Another consequence of higher sea levels is the intrusion of salt into groundwater which, in some places, affects groundwater supplies as far as 50 kilometers inland. This not only has a damaging effect on farming but also endangers drinking water supplies.

Ecological systems in coastal regions are particularly valuable and species-rich; people are, generally, attracted to these regions, thus making them popular tourist destinations. Who doesn't savor the thought of strolling along a sandy beach, looking for sea shells, casting dreamy glances over the water while watching seagulls and terns? The more fortunate among us might have already been able to observe seals, whales or dolphins off the coast, been snorkeling among brightly-colored fish in a coral reef, or have witnessed a large, old sea turtle making its way up the beach in the middle of a tropical night to dig a nest above the waterline and lay its eggs.

However, rising sea levels intensify the special risks faced by these ecosystems (discussed further in subsequent chapters). Areas at risk include, for example, wetlands and salt marshes, coral reefs and mangrove forests. The coral reefs of today have established themselves during the past few thousand years – after the period of melting of the enormous ice sheets of the last ice age had finished and the sea levels had stabilized at a more or less constant level. Tropical coral reefs are thought to offer a home to more species of marine life than any other marine ecosystem; estimates place the number of species living on, around, or off these reefs at between 0.5 and 2 million. For around 100 million people, they provide an income through tourism or fishing and they also protect the coast against erosion and tsunamis. Research carried out in the aftermath of the devastating tsunami which struck around Christmas 2004 showed that the distance the flood waves were able to penetrate inland was greatly reduced in coastal areas which were protected by intact coral reefs or mangrove forests.

In shallow waters, warm water corals flourish just below the surface – this is because the ecosystem requires sunlight to grow. Coral reefs can adapt to changes in sea level by growing upward. However, empirical data has shown that, under favorable conditions (i.e. ignoring the stress factors like warming and acidification which we will discuss further below), corals can only keep up with a maximum sea level rise of 10 mm per year. This raises serious questions as to whether the coral will be able to keep up with the expected acceleration in sea level rises later this century.

Mangrove forests (see Plate 7 in the color section), which presently line 8% of the world's coastlines, are also able to adapt only within certain limits. A detailed scenario analysis for these forests has shown that even a sea level rise of 50 cm by the year 2100 would probably spell the end for around a quarter of all coastal mangrove forests.

So is a further rise in sea levels unavoidable, or can we still stop the trend? Actually, this is the wrong way to put the question, since there is no definitive answer. Instead, we should be asking: how much further sea level rise is already unavoidable?

If we just take a look at the physics involved, a further slight increase in sea levels is unavoidable, presumably in the region of a few tens of centimeters or possibly even less than 10 centimeters. If we were to stop all emissions of carbon dioxide and other greenhouse gases tomorrow, then the concentration of CO_2 could start to drop again immediately. With a certain time lag, the global temperature would also gradually start to drop, returning to approximately 1950 levels by the year 2100. There would be a strong slowing in the rise of sea levels and, from the next century or the next century after that, sea levels would start to drop again.

Both politically and economically, however, this is a drastic scenario that is completely unrealistic. Nevertheless, even more realistic and effective mitigation (climate protection) scenarios, for example a model proposed by the Swedish energy professor Christian Azar, would limit further global warming in this century to less than 1 °C and subsequently allow temperatures to cool down again, which would probably mean a further rise in sea levels of a few tens of centimeters over the course of several centuries. With the aid of suitable adaptation measures, this level of rise would be one we could cope with.

If, however, nothing is done to mitigate climate change, and we allow emissions to increase unchecked, then global sea level would probably rise by several meters during the course of the next few centuries.

This gives us a clear choice: a rise in sea levels either of a few tens of centimeters or of several meters. Our generation has the historic responsibility of taking this decision. Our path will be determined in the next ten or twenty years, as this is the time in which decisions will be taken about the energy system that will serve us for the next fifty years or so. The future of the oceans is in our hands.

In 2006, the German Advisory Council on Global Change (WBGU) presented an assessment of the oceans in which so-called "guard rails" were proposed for sea level, i.e. limits which should not be exceeded. According to the proposal, a rise of more than one meter over pre-industrial levels should be avoided in the long term (i.e. over several centuries), and the rate of sea level rise should be kept below 5 cm per decade. With this special report, the WBGU hopes to stimulate a broad discussion about meaningful limits for how much we raise sea levels. People can – and should – debate whether the proposed numbers are too high or too low, but it would definitely be irresponsible to just stick our heads in the sand and ignore the problem of rising sea levels.

We have to face up to the consequences of our actions and make a responsible decision about what we regard as being an acceptable rise in sea levels. This needs to be considered hand-in-hand with the levels of CO_2 emissions this society will allow.

Tropical cyclones

2005 was a record year for tropical cyclones. The devastation caused by Hurricane Katrina in New Orleans (with a death toll of at least 1836) alerted many people to the risks posed by such storms. The development of these tropical cyclones is so closely linked to the oceans that no book about the oceans would be complete without a discussion of this topic. Tropical cyclones develop out of a disturbance – usually simply a thunderstorm – over the tropical oceans. Warm and humid air rises and cools along the way – causing the water vapor to condense. The heat released during the condensation process causes a continued rapid upward motion of the air – similar to a chimney – as this "built-in heating" continually keeps the air warmer than the air around it. The "fuel" which powers this chimney – i.e. the source of energy – is, ultimately, the warm seawater. Close to the surface of the ocean, air flows from all directions into the center of the disturbance, where it then replaces the rising air. The Earth's rotation (or, more specifically, the Coriolis force) causes this air to be deflected and the system starts to rotate. The result is an organized rotating system which can be sustained for several days until it runs out of fuel (i.e. when the tropical cyclone moves over colder waters or land) or until it is torn apart by unfavorable wind shear.

The Coriolis force vanishes in the immediate vicinity of the equator and, as a result, no tropical cyclones can occur there.

However, away from the equator, tropical cyclones can develop anywhere where the water temperatures exceed 26.5 °C. In the Atlantic and the Northeast Pacific, tropical cyclones above a specific strength (a wind speed of 118 km/h) are traditionally referred to as hurricanes, while the same cyclones are known as typhoons in the Northwest Pacific or just simply cyclones anywhere else. Every year, an average of eighty tropical cyclones travel across the world's oceans, 11% of these are in the North Atlantic and just over half of which reach hurricane strength. Fortunately, only very few reach a coastline – where and when this happens is largely a question of chance.

The 2004 season was a major year for tropical cyclones, with a number of events making the headlines: for the first time ever, a hurricane appeared in the South Atlantic, Florida was hit by a record four hurricanes in a single year, and – again for the first time – Japan was hit by ten typhoons in one season. However, this was topped by the events of 2005. Since records began in 1851, there had never been as many tropical cyclones (twenty-eight against a previous record of twenty-one), never before did so many reach full hurricane strength (fifteen against a previous record of eleven), and never before had there been three category-5 hurricanes – the worst category. In addition, Hurricane Wilma was the most intense hurricane ever measured, with a central pressure of just 882 mb (millibar) measured on October 19. In this same year, Hurricane Vince marked the first time ever that a tropical cyclone formed close to Europe. It developed into a hurricane-strength cyclone close to Madeira on October 9, before moving over the mainland in Spain, though, fortunately, in a weakened state.

In contrast, 2006 was a comparatively calm year. There were nine tropical cyclones, five of which reached hurricane strength. This corresponds almost exactly to the long-term average. On the other hand, in the Western Pacific, the number of tropical cyclones was above average with 15 typhoons, including seven particularly severe "super typhoons." In August, 2006, Typhoon Saomai left 458 people dead in the Philippines and China. In May 2008, the category-4 Typhoon Nargis struck the coast of Burma, causing over 100,000 casualties.

What conclusions can we draw from these developments? Do the records broken in 2005 offer any proof for climate change? Or, conversely, does the comparatively "normal" year, 2006, offer evidence that there is, in fact, no trend towards more severe tropical cyclones? Both of these conclusions would, of course, be wrong. It is scientifically impossible to draw any conclusions about long-term developments from individual years or an individual storm such as Katrina, although this type of event, naturally, plays very heavily on the imagination of the public. The same applies for tropical storms as for ocean temperatures and sea levels: any long-term trend will be subject to the superimposed effects of short-term natural fluctuations and, in the case of cyclone activity, these fluctuations can be very large from one year to the next.

To draw conclusions about climate trends and, therefore, possible man-made contributions to these trends, it is not sufficient to consider individual years. Instead, we need to look at sets of data which cover the longest possible period of time. A different way of looking at this would be to attempt to find out whether a dice had secretly been manipulated to throw twice as many sixes as "normal." If we roll three sixes in a row with this dice, then this is by no means proof that something is wrong with the dice. Conversely, the fact that it is possible to roll three sixes in a row even with a normal dice is not enough to prove that our dice has *not* been tampered with. Even a dice which has been rigged to throw sixes will occasionally return a one. The facts of the matter are very straightforward when considering the dice. Nonetheless, this is precisely the type of argument that is frequently presented in the media in relation to tropical cyclones – for example, when commentators point out that there have been worse hurricanes than Katrina in the past. This is true but it tells us little about whether or not this type of storm is becoming more frequent or not.

Do we have any information on the long-term trends for tropical cyclones? In terms of the total number of storms worldwide, no clear trend is yet evident, although the frequency of cyclones in the Atlantic has clearly been above average during the last ten years. Analyses of satellite data and measurements taken from aircraft do, however, indicate a marked increase in the *strength* of tropical cyclones since 1970 (see Fig. 4.7).

In 2008, a reanalysis of all global satellite data since 1980 was published. This found that world-wide the number of tropical storms remained constant. However, the strongest storms have increased markedly in intensity. A 1 °C warming would correspond to an about 30% increase in the number of tropical storms of the strongest categories 4 and 5. These results are plausible, in that *a priori* there is no clear physical reason why the total number of storms should increase in a warmer climate; their formation is a matter of weather and thus chance. There is, however, a good reason why storms should grow to stronger wind speeds in a warmer climate: warmer ocean temperatures are able to provide more energy input to these storms. Given that these are very new results, no consensus has been reached and the debate about these data will no doubt continue for some years to come.

Nevertheless, if we assume that the essence of these data analyses is correct and that the strength of tropical cyclones has, indeed, increased, then this leads us to the following question:

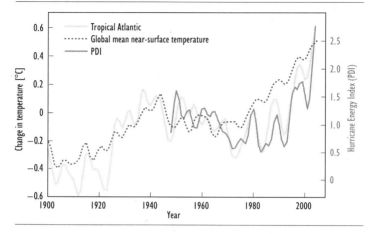

Figure 4.7 Change in the energy of hurricanes in the Atlantic (gray)
          compared to the water temperatures in the tropical Atlantic
          (light blue) and the global average temperature (dotted line)

what is the reason for this trend? Everything points towards the
culprit being the steadily increasing temperatures in the tropical
oceans. This increase has been 0.5 °C in the last thirty years. The
fact that warmer water contributes to the formation of stronger
tropical cyclones is undisputed. There are other factors alongside
the water temperatures, which can influence tropical cyclones, in
particular certain aspects of atmospheric circulation like wind
shear. For example, the occurrence of an El Niño event in the
Pacific in 2006 slowed down the formation of Atlantic hurricanes
thanks to the resulting unfavorable (for hurricane formation)
wind conditions. But the distinction between long-term trends
and short-term fluctuations is again crucial here. Of all of the
factors that influence hurricane formation, it is only the ocean
temperature which displays a long-term trend, while the other

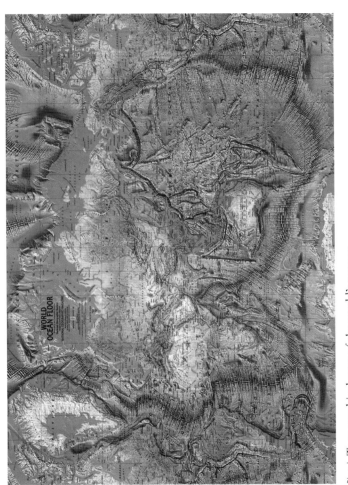

Plate 1 Topographical map of the world's oceans.

Plate 2 The ocean is in constant exchange with the atmosphere. It is the water source for most of the world's clouds and precipitation.

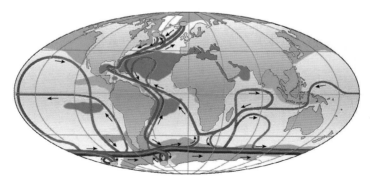

Plate 3 The thermohaline circulation of the world's oceans (simplified). The surface currents are in red, deep currents in blue and bottom currents in violet. Yellow dots mark the areas where deep water forms.

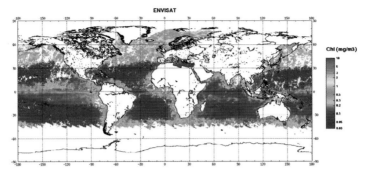

Plate 4 Satellite image of the distribution of the plant pigment, chlorophyll, in the surface waters of the world's oceans. The image is an average for the month of May.

Plate 5 The microscopic phytoplankton in the ocean. The photograph shows phytoplankton caught in the North Sea with a net in spring. Photo: N. Nichols

Plate 6 The *Calanus finmarchicus*. Maximum size 5mm.

Plate 7 Mangrove forests still line many coasts such as here on the Caribbean island of Hispanola. However, they are endangered by land clearance and the rising sea levels.

factors appear to fluctuate more or less randomly. As a result, when we compare data averaged over several years (as shown in Fig. 4.7), we see a clear correlation between hurricane strength and sea surface temperatures.

The final question to ask, then, is whether or not the rise in tropical ocean temperatures during the last few decades has been caused predominantly by the effects of human activities. From a climatological point of view, everything points in this direction. Tropical oceans have heated up to the same degree and with a similar time evolution to the global average temperatures. There is no physical reason why they would be spared the effects of rising CO_2 concentrations. In computer simulations of the anthropogenic impact on climate, predictions of how the tropical oceans should warm up match what is actually observed. By contrast, the evidence for a "natural cycle" of temperatures in the Atlantic which is being invoked by some hurricane researchers is weak – recent analyses carried out by US researchers Mike Mann and Kevin Trenberth came to the conclusion that the alleged cycle in the temperatures shown in Fig. 4.7 is probably deceptive. In reality, what we see is a temporary cooling resulting from aerosol pollution between 1940 and 1970.

In summary, we can therefore conclude that it is probable that the strength of tropical cyclones has increased during the last thirty years, and it is very probable that this is a consequence of rising sea surface temperatures. The oceans in turn are heating up further primarily because of the effects of the anthropogenic greenhouse effect.

More scientific analysis is certainly required to resolve the data quality issue – and although it is very improbable that the strength of tropical cyclones has not increased, corrections to the magnitude of the observed trends may be required in the light of further studies. The extent of this increase is also unclear from a theoretical point of view, as the observed increase in hurricane strength is significantly greater than that predicted by theory. If we are lucky, then this discrepancy will turn out to be a result of data-related problems. In which case, we can hope that the mathematical models which predict only a small future increase in cyclone activity will turn out to be correct. If, however, we are less fortunate, then the relationship may indeed be as pronounced as shown in Fig. 4.7 and continue in this way in the future. In this case, the expected further increase in ocean temperatures would dramatically amplify the hurricane risks.

This aside, and even if the strength of the tropical cyclones remains unchanged, we can still expect a significant increase in damage resulting from these storms. The reasons for this are threefold. Firstly, more and more people are choosing to live in vulnerable coastal areas. Secondly, as was already explained above, sea levels are rising and this increases the level of risk posed to coasts by hurricanes. As IPCC chairman Pachauri rightly noted in the aftermath of Typhoon Nargis, the damage would have been significantly smaller had sea levels not already risen by 20 centimeters. Finally, in a warmer climate, the volume of rain associated with cyclones will increase because warmer air can contain more water than cold. A large proportion of cyclone damage is caused by the flooding associated with the heavy rainfall rather than by the powerful winds. Ultimately, it is also possible that the regions affected by tropical cyclones could be widened as a consequence of the warming of the oceans – examples which support this hypothesis include the hurricane in the South Atlantic in 2004 and Hurricane Vince in 2005. Sadly, all of these reasons lead us to believe that tropical cyclones will continue to make the headlines in the future.

We have concentrated here on tropical cyclones, as they represent a phenomenon which is largely caused by the oceans and, therefore, fit very well into a book about the oceans. However, at this point readers might also be wondering about extratropical storms – the kind that typically hit the coasts of Western Europe in winter. Unfortunately, climate researchers have not yet been able to draw any clear conclusions about the future development of these storms, as conflicting trends act upon them in the mid-latitudes. For example, the particularly pronounced warming of the North Pole reduces the temperature difference between the equator and the high latitudes, which should, theoretically, reduce the severity of the storms. On the other hand, the stratosphere is cooling, which increases the vertical temperature gradients and could, therefore, have the opposite effect and make storms more severe. These are only two of several factors. Climate models and even the higher-resolution weather forecasting models are particularly poor at predicting the wind speeds of the strongest storms. It is still unclear whether extratropical storms will tend to increase or decrease globally. Furthermore, when we look at a particular region, it is also less important whether there is a global increase or decrease, as it is, instead, more important how the tracks of cyclones shift. With a look to Europe, we can expect that the tracks of the Atlantic low pressure system will probably tend to shift northward, with the result that there will be more storms in northern Europe and fewer in southern Europe in the future.

Changes to the ocean currents

One particular scenario which is always a dramatic favorite in the media is the risk of a "shutdown of the Gulf Stream," which could even trigger a "new Ice Age," at least according to some reports. In the Hollywood blockbuster, *The Day after Tomorrow*,

directed by Roland Emmerich, this scenario was used as the basis
for a science fiction story in which New York is simultaneously
buried by snow storms and flooded by a tsunami, while the US
government retreats to the comparative safety of Mexico. Of
course, nobody would confuse this exciting Hollywood thriller
with a documentary but with some of the reports we see in the
media, it is much harder to separate serious scientific principles
from fiction and exaggeration.

The basic principles of the Gulf Stream and thermohaline
circulation in the oceans were already covered in Chapter 1. We
saw there that the Gulf Stream is primarily wind-driven and that
it is part of a system of large subtropical gyres. Accordingly, it
could never shut down as long as the winds continue to blow
(which there is no doubt they will). Reports in the media about
its demise can simply be boiled down to a lack of accuracy in the
terminology used. Oceanographers distinguish between the Gulf
Stream in the western Atlantic and its extended arm, the North
Atlantic Current, which flows in the north-eastern Atlantic up
to the coasts of Europe. The North Atlantic Current could,
indeed, shut down. As a lot of people tend to lump these currents together and refer to them jointly as the Gulf Stream (this
is sometimes done in school atlases as well), journalists often
simplify the story and tell us that the Gulf Stream could shut
down. Of course this is not correct, because even in this popular
nomenclature only part of the Gulf Stream would shut down.
For years, we have been trying to get journalists to use the term
North Atlantic Current instead of Gulf Stream but they, generally, prefer the better-known term, believing that anything else
would be too much for their readers. (Hollywood, thankfully,
doesn't seem to agree, as the Emmerich film mentioned above
speaks consistently of the North Atlantic Current.)

Is there, then, a real risk of the North Atlantic Current

shutting down? Already in the 1960s, the American Henry Stommel, one of the pioneers of modern oceanography, discovered on the basis of some simple theoretical considerations that the thermohaline circulation of the Atlantic should have a critical point (in the modern jargon of non-linear dynamics, this is referred to as a "bifurcation") at which it could tip from one state to another. The reason for this is a feedback effect with the salt content: the way in which the thermohaline circulation works (which, at the surface, the North Atlantic Current also forms part of) is that heavy, salty water sinks down in the north. However, the water there is only salty enough for this to happen because this flow carries salt from the subtropics. Salt enables the flow of water, and the current delivers salt – this is a cycle which keeps itself going. If it is perturbed enough – for example by adding some fresh water – then it could be interrupted. The current would weaken, the supply of salt would break down, and a freshwater "lid" would spread over the North Atlantic and prevent water from sinking and, hence, the formation of deep water.

This type of tipping of the current – initially little more than idle speculation – was then used in the 1980s by American ocean researcher Wally Broecker to explain abrupt climate changes in Earth's history. As was explained in Chapter 1, sediment data has since confirmed that, at least during the last ice age, such abrupt ocean circulation changes did indeed take place repeatedly. Broecker raised the question: under what conditions could this type of situation arise again in the future, possibly triggered by the growing man-made interference with the climate system?

Global warming could disturb the sinking of deep water, and therefore the entire thermohaline circulation system in two ways. Firstly, the warming of the surface waters makes it more difficult for water to sink, as warmer water is lighter than colder water. Secondly, the warming brings more precipitation into the higher latitudes, as a result of which more freshwater is carried to the sea through rivers (this trend has already been measured) and the melting of ice adds even more fresh water to the sea. All this causes a reduction in the salinity of the North Atlantic surface waters – this, too, is a sustained trend which has been observed for decades. However, according to model calculations, this reduction in salinity is still too small to have a noticeable impact on the current.

The key questions we need to address are the following: how much fresh water would need to be added to the ocean to bring the current to a standstill? And how much fresh water can we expect to be added to the ocean in this region in the future if global warming continues unchecked? Unfortunately, we cannot answer either of these questions with a great degree of accuracy. Models and data from climate history indicate that the addition of around 100,000 m³ per second would probably represent a critical amount – but this is only a rough estimate of an order of magnitude for the amount of fresh water required to change the current patterns. The amount of fresh water we can expect to be added to the sea in the future depends, in particular, on the melting of the ice sheet in Greenland and, as discussed above, it is difficult to make reliable predictions about this. If all of this ice was to melt over the course of 1000 years, this would result in an average outflow of meltwater of 100,000 m³ per second. As a rule, this is not included in the current climate models, so these models are not really any use for predicting the fate of the North Atlantic Current. In view of these uncertainties, we can presently only conclude that there is a risk, but one which is very difficult to quantify. The latest IPCC report published in 2007 gives the risk of a major abrupt ocean circulation change by the year 2100 as less than 10%. This is hardly reassuring, as one would prefer to rule out such a major risk at a one-in-a-million level, similar to the risk of a nuclear accident.

What would the consequences be if the North Atlantic Current did shut down? The "Ice Age" often mentioned in the media would certainly not be one of them. Back in the mid-1990s, we pointed out in a number of publications that global warming (which, after all, is what causes these scenarios) would probably more than compensate for any cooling due to the missing heat otherwise transported by this current system. There are only a few, very specific conditions under which parts of Europe could become colder than they are today. Firstly, if – contrary to expectations – the current were to change abruptly as early as the middle of the 21st century (as forecast in a Dutch simulation model, which predicted significant cooling over Scandinavia as a result). Or secondly, if the North Atlantic Current shut down permanently and global temperatures were to go down again, due to the concentration of greenhouse gases in the atmosphere dropping again in the next few centuries (this is quite a realistic scenario). This could leave the north-western part of Europe several degrees colder in the long run, after the greenhouse warming has subsided.

The more important and direct consequences of a shutdown – or, to a lesser extent, of a weakening – of the North Atlantic Current would not actually be changes in temperature. Marine life would be affected most directly. It is precisely the thermohaline circulation of the North Atlantic which makes it one of the most fertile and fish-rich high sea regions on Earth. Initial model calculations predict that a weakening of this circulation would have a huge adverse effect on ecosystems in the Atlantic. Changes to the current would also affect regional sea levels, as discussed above. Model simulation show that a shut-down of the thermohaline circulation would lead to a rise in sea levels in the North

Atlantic by up to 1 meter – and this rise would be in addition to the global rise in sea levels already taking place. Furthermore, these dynamic changes would take place quickly, as they would follow the changes to the current system without any time lag. In contrast, sea levels in the southern hemisphere would fall slightly (or the effects of the global sea level rise would be reduced), as this dynamic redistribution of sea water adds up to zero in the global average.

Another important consequence of the thermohaline circulation shutting down would probably be a shift of the tropical rain belt (the "Intertropical Convergence Zone"), which is normally located at the so-called thermal equator. The northern hemisphere is, normally, slightly warmer than the southern hemisphere, as the thermohaline circulation transports vast amounts of heat across the equator to the north. As a consequence, the thermal equator is slightly north of the geographical equator. If this current stops, then the thermal equator would shift towards the south. This would probably result in dramatic changes to precipitation patterns in, for example, southern China, something which is supported by data from climate history. This is what happened during abrupt ocean circulation changes during the last Ice Age.

Are there already any indications that changes are occurring in the North Atlantic Current? British researchers headed by Harry Bryden made the headlines in 2005 when they interpreted some ocean measurements as evidence for a 30% reduction in the Atlantic overturning circulation over the last fifty years. Many of their colleagues in the scientific community are skeptical about these conclusions, and the scientists themselves have now downscaled them, but they remain convinced that a weakening has occurred, albeit to a lesser degree than originally claimed. The reason that this type of discussion takes place is that there is a lack of reliable long-term data, particularly for the deeper ocean layers.

Because of this, an attempt was made to estimate the strength of the current indirectly from the difference in surface temperatures between the South Atlantic and the North Atlantic. From this, it was concluded that the strength of the current had decreased between the 1940s and 1970s, which was then followed by a period of recovery. The basic idea behind this approach is plausible, because it is precisely this current that causes the North Atlantic to be warmer than the South Atlantic. However, there are a number of other factors which also influence this temperature difference, in particular the cooling effects of aerosol pollution in the atmosphere which we have already discussed and which saw a great increase particularly in the northern hemisphere precisely between the 1940s and 1970s, but which have been decreasing again ever since. Unfortunately, we must therefore conclude that we are largely ignorant about how our huge Atlantic overturning, the thermohaline circulation, has changed during previous decades. International measurement programs which have started up in recent years offer some hope, however, that we will at least be better informed about future changes – provided funding cuts do not close down these programs again after a few years.

Methane release from the sea bed?

There is one final danger associated with the oceans as a result of climate change that we would like to address in this chapter: the release of methane from the sea bed. The sea bed contains huge carbon deposits in the form of methane hydrate – as an order of magnitude, the quantities involved are comparable to the global coal reserves. Methane hydrate has the appearance of slushy ice but it can be burned. It is a mixture of methane and water, which can form a crystaline structure under very high pressure and at low temperatures, at which point it then becomes solid. The conditions under which methane hydrate is stable are generally given in sea beds below a depth of 500 meters but, in Arctic waters, it can also exist closer to the surface.

Most of this methane has accumulated in the sea bed over a period of millions of years, where it is a waste product created by life in the ocean: it is actually dead biomass, which sediments and is decomposed by bacteria. In some regions, such as the Gulf of Mexico, methane can also seep up from natural gas deposits under the sea, which then combines to hydrate with water in the sediment. The problem here is that, as a consequence of climate change, ocean water is also becoming warmer – and, albeit with a time lag of a few centuries, this also applies to deep water in regions containing methane hydrate deposits. Ultimately, the layer of sediment containing the hydrates will also warm up. As a result, some of the methane will change state and become gaseous. This is because the zone in the sediment with the right conditions for methane hydrate to remain stable will shrink under the effects of warming.

There are now two possible scenarios. The first one is a sudden, episodic release of methane. This could happen if, due to the destabilization of the methane, landslides occur on the sea bed. This scenario is more than just fantasy: today, we still find the tell-tale signs which show instances of this type of landslide throughout the Earth's history. One famous example is the Storegga Slide off the coast of Norway, an event which took place around 8000 years ago and caused a massive tsunami which hit the Shetland Islands with a height of at least 25 meters and was still 5 meters high when it reached the coast of Britain. Although the amount of methane released in the process – one gigaton – was huge, this was still not enough to have a notable effect on the climate, despite the fact that methane is a very potent greenhouse gas. This example illustrates that, although this type of landslide can cause a devastating flood wave, it does not have a big impact on climate, even in an extreme case such as this.

However, the situation is quite different in the second scenario: a gradual release of methane. To understand this, it is best to imagine that the warming of the global oceans causes steadily increasing amounts of methane to gradually bubble up out of the sea bed in tiny bubbles. Initially, most of the methane is dissolved in ocean water. Some escapes into the atmosphere, where it oxidizes and forms CO_2. The part remaining in the water also oxidizes, again forming CO_2. The consequences of this would be twofold: firstly, the ocean water would become more acidic (see Chapter 5) and, secondly, it would represent a continuous source of CO_2 for the atmosphere for many thousands of years to come, which would increase the greenhouse effect. Model calculations performed by American ocean expert David Archer have illustrated the potential order of magnitude of this problem. According to his conclusions, this mechanism could approximately double the effects of our fossil-fuel era on atmospheric CO_2 concentrations for thousands of years to come. Accordingly, this is not an acute problem which will affect us in the next century, but instead it is a creeping long-term consequence for the climate on Earth. However, this problem does make it very clear that our actions in this century may instigate processes in the world's oceans which could have a knock-on effect for many thousands of years, and which may therefore change our planet in a strong and lasting way.

5 Changes to the Element Cycles

There are a number of element cycles which characterize – and in turn are influenced by – the ocean and its biology. Three of these cycles were presented in Chapter 3. The fact that we focus on them in this book stems from the fact that they are dramatically influenced by human activities. In the case of carbon and nitrogen, the changes occurring in the global distribution and recirculation of the elements have major implications on how the oceans function and their future. Finally, we will also take a look at the sulfur cycle here because the oceans represent an important source of this element. Here again, changes can take place as shifts in the carbon and nitrogen cycles feed back into the sulfur cycle.

Phosphorus and silicon

At this juncture, however, it is appropriate to devote some of our attention to two other elements whose cycles are relevant to the ability of the oceans to function in their normal way, namely phosphorus and silicon. Phosphorus is an important nutrient which is absolutely crucial to a number of cell processes. In fact, when we talk about the nutrients required for phytoplankton growth and photosynthesis, we always mean a combination of nitrogen and phosphorus together.

In freshwater systems, availability of phosphorus is usually considered to be the limiting factor for plant growth. However, in most marine systems, it is believed that nitrogen is the nutrient which controls phytoplankton growth. This is one of the reasons why we will concentrate more on nitrogen here than phosphorus, but another is the fact that the changes to the oceanic phosphorus cycle appear to have far less dramatic consequences than those of the carbon and nitrogen cycles. Whilst it is true that the annual influx of phosphorus has increased by a factor of more than two worldwide, as a result of human population growth and human activities in recent history, the impact of this phosphorus enrichment on global ocean processes appears to be rather less than the impact of anthropogenic carbon and nitrogen enrichment.

Of course, large quantities of phosphorus originating from human activities reach coastal regions of oceans with waste water, although there is, however, some good news on that front: waste water treatment plants are now proving to be effective at removing phosphorus. In most industrialized nations, there has actually been a decrease in the water-borne introduction of phosphorus into the marine environment in recent decades thanks to the treatment of waste water. Of course, phosphorus enrichment still occurs in many coastal waters – even in regions with effective waste-water treatment plants – and this enrichment can become an important factor which impacts on local biological conditions. Furthermore, it appears that the available amounts of phosphorus may play a role in the fixation of nitrogen in the open ocean.

The silicon cycle is also an important factor in the oceans' ability to function in their normal way. However, similarly to phosphorus, the role of the ocean in the cycles of these elements is not impacted as dramatically by human activities as is the case with the carbon, nitrogen and, possibly, sulfur cycles. Silicon (Si) is a component in the shells of diatoms. Diatoms (and a number of marine animals) clearly, therefore, have a requirement for this element. They also play an important role in the transport of silicon from surface waters to ocean sediment. A change in silicon availability could, therefore, potentially lead to a decrease in the numbers of diatoms living in the oceans. As diatoms are a particularly important factor in ensuring the functioning of the biological pump, which transports organic carbon from the surface to the bottom water layers of the ocean (see Chapter 3), a change in their abundance may have consequences for the cycles of other elements. It does, indeed, appear that there has been a decrease in the relative abundance of silicon in the oceans as a consequence of human activities.

Most silicon is transported to the ocean in rivers and streams, and the construction of ever more dams means that the water spends more time in these systems. This extra time gives the diatoms living there more time to take up silicon. Therefore, instead of being transported to the ocean, a greater proportion of the silicon is fixed biologically in the rivers and falls to the river-bed. Theoretically, this change in the way silicon is transported to the oceans could have affected the abundance of diatoms there. However, neither the available data nor our understanding of the factors controlling the relative distributions of different phyto-plankton groups are sufficient to determine whether or not this has been the case.

Clearly, phosphorus and silicon are important for phytoplank-ton and the cycles of both of these elements have been altered by human activities. However, it is not yet clear whether the conse-quences for these cycles are so serious that we truly can speak of a global impact on the oceans. In this respect, the situation is very different for these two elements than it is for the carbon and nitrogen cycles.

Carbon

Let us now look at carbon. The most obvious change is a redistribution of this element between the individual reservoirs in the cycle. As was already discussed in Chapter 4, increasingly more CO_2 is accumulating in the atmosphere. By analyzing CO_2 concentrations in air bubbles trapped inside the Antarctic ice sheet, scientists have managed to map the concentration of CO_2 in the atmosphere over the last approximately 650,000 years (a portion of this time series is shown in Fig. 5.1).

The concentration has fluctuated throughout the entire period. Changes have been relatively gradual, however, and the CO_2 concentration has remained within a range from about 180 parts per million (ppm) to 280 ppm – with the exception of the last century. At present (2008), the CO_2 concentration in the atmosphere is 385 ppm, and the Intergovernmental Panel on Climate Change (IPCC) and others predict that the concentration will exceed a value of 700 ppm by the year 2100 if anthropogenic release of CO_2 to the atmosphere continues at its present rate. This estimate means that the carbon dioxide concentration will have nearly tripled over a period of approximately 200 years by the beginning of the next century. There is no evidence for such a rapid rate of increase in the geological data from Earth's climate history – indeed, it may be completely unique in the entire history of the Earth.

Where does all of this additional CO_2 originate from? It does not come from an introduction of more carbon into the global cycle per se but, rather, from a redistribution of carbon between the different reservoirs illustrated in Fig. 3.1 (in Chapter 3). A large part of it is the result of the transfer of carbon from the huge fossil deposits in the sediments under the current and prehistoric oceans. Without human intervention, these deposits are relatively stable and there is little transfer of carbon from them

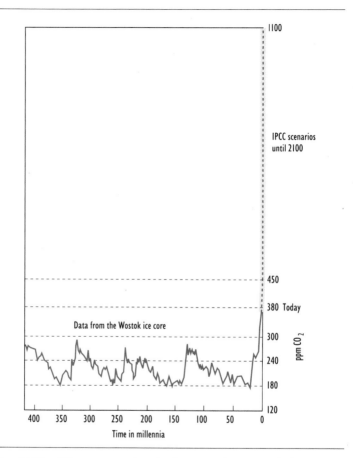

Figure 5.1 The CO_2 concentrations in the atmosphere over the last
450,000 years

The earlier values are based on the gas concentrations in bubbles of the ice cores
from Antarctica. Direct measurements exist since the middle of the last century.
The IPCC estimates for the period until 2100 follow on from the curve of these
measurements.

to the atmosphere. However, through the burning of fossil fuels (oil, gas, and coal), human activity is releasing carbon from these stable reserves and transferring it in the form of CO_2 (a product of combustion) into the atmosphere. While the burning of fossil fuels is the main reason for the man-made increase in CO_2 levels, it is not the only one. Interventions into the vegetation cover, such as felling and burning of forests, also contribute to this increase by decreasing the removal of CO_2 from the atmosphere.

The consequences of the increased CO_2 concentration

This redistribution of carbon in the various areas of the Earth System has a number of consequences for the system as a whole. The most immediate impact affects most people via the greenhouse effect of CO_2 (see Chapter 4). Our world is heated up by the sun. If the Earth does not have a mechanism to get rid of this heat again, then it will simply get hotter and hotter. One of the mechanisms by which the Earth loses this heat is through the emission of infrared radiation. However, CO_2 is one of a number of gases which make the atmosphere less permeable to infrared radiation. Thus, the more carbon dioxide that is present in the atmosphere, the more of the heat leaving the surface of the Earth becomes absorbed and retained in the atmosphere – and, as a result, the climate heats up.

According to predictions, this global warming will alter the role of the oceans in the global carbon cycle, as less phytoplankton photosynthesis will occur and, hence, the amount of carbon that can be biologically converted into organic material will be reduced. To understand why global warming is expected to result in a reduction in phytoplankton activity, it is necessary to refer back to some of the concepts presented in Chapter 2.

For the most part, the ocean is stratified in stable layers. This means that there are relatively warm surface layers above one or more colder layers further down in the water column. Nutrients sink in the form of biological particles from the surface to bottom waters and, in order for plants to grow in the light-rich surface waters of the ocean, nutrients must be transported back from deep waters to the surface. This transport of nutrients requires the addition of energy to the system – energy that can break down the water column stratification and mix the nutrient-rich bottom water into the surface layers of the ocean.

With warmer air temperatures, the surface layers of the ocean will also become warmer. Therefore, the temperature difference between the surface and deeper layers of the ocean will be greater. Consequently, the stratification of the water column will also be greater and it will require more energy to mix nutrient-rich bottom water into the upper reaches of the water column, where light is sufficient to support photosynthesis (the so-called euphotic zone). The fact that more energy will be required to mix surface and bottom waters in a warmer Earth System means that the water is likely to be less well mixed than is the case today.

It is predicted that there will be a reduction in the transport of nutrients from bottom waters to surface waters of the ocean. However, phytoplankton require these nutrients in order to carry out photosynthesis. Fewer nutrients in the upper layers will, therefore, mean less photosynthesis and less incorporation of CO_2 into biological (organic) material. As a further consequence, if less carbon is incorporated into organic matter then there will also be less food available for the non-photosynthesizing marine organisms such as fish. Likewise, there will be less material available in the biological and carbonate pumps, which transport carbon from surface waters to deeper regions of the ocean. Thus, a simple shift in temperature is enough to adversely affect the carbon cycle in the ocean. As the oceans play an important role in the global carbon cycle, this means that the overall global cycle will be changed.

Acidification of surface waters

There is, however, another very important change that the increased concentration of CO_2 in the atmosphere is predicted to bring about in terms of life in the oceans and the role of the oceans in the carbon cycle. As was described in Chapter 3, the surface water in the oceans and the atmosphere are in contact with one another over approximately 70% of the Earth's surface, and gaseous carbon dioxide exists in both. When two media (in this case, air and water) are in contact with each another, the gases on either side of the boundary surface constantly try to establish an equilibrium. Accordingly, if the CO_2 concentration in the atmosphere increases, the carbon dioxide content of the surface waters will also increase.

As a result of this tendency to establish a gas equilibrium between air and water, the Earth's oceans have already taken up around 30 to 50% of the "extra" man-made CO_2. This means, of course, that the actual measured concentration of CO_2 in the atmosphere is lower than it would be if there were no oceans. The oceans have, therefore, actually slowed global warming by taking up some of the CO_2 which otherwise would be in the atmosphere. Few people are aware of the tremendous service carried out for us by the oceans, in terms of influencing the environment we experience.

What happens when CO_2 enters a water-based liquid? The short answer is that the liquid becomes more acidic. We experience this with carbonated drinks. This is why dentists warn against excessive consumption of drinks like cola – their acidity dissolves some of the components in tooth enamel. What actually happens when CO_2 is dissolved in water is that carbonic acid is formed: the CO_2 reacts with the water (H_2O) and forms carbonic acid, H_2CO_3. This molecule disassociates in solution; protons (H+) are released and HCO_3- is formed. The number of free (unattached) protons in a liquid determines its acidity. The more protons present, the more acidic a water-based liquid becomes.

Acidity is normally measured and expressed on a "pH scale," which is simply a (logarithmic) expression of the number of free protons present in the liquid. One might, therefore, expect liquids with a higher acidity to also have a higher pH value. Unfortunately, thanks to the vagaries of logarithms and the logic of the founder of the scale (Søren P.L. Sørensen, a Danish biochemist), this is not the case. In fact, a lower pH value actually means an increase in acidity.

As a consequence of the increased concentration of CO_2 in the atmosphere, a lowering of the pH value of surface waters (i.e. increasing acidification) of the ocean is predicted and, indeed in some areas, has already been observed. Thus, the surface waters of the ocean are, just like carbonated drinks, becoming more acidic through the addition of more CO_2. This demonstrates that global changes resulting from human activities – in this case the increasing concentration of CO_2 in the atmosphere – cause more than just climate change.

As the equilibrium of concentrations of a gas on either side of a boundary surface follows relatively simple chemical principles, it is possible to predict future pH values on the basis of different concentrations of atmospheric CO_2. When/if atmospheric CO_2 concentrations exceed 1000 ppm (which is possible by the year 2100 if CO_2 emissions continue to increase), it is predicted that the pH value of the surface waters in the oceans will have decreased by about 0.5 pH points. This may not sound like much. However, because the pH scale is logarithmic, a change by 0.5 pH points actually corresponds to a tripling of the number of free protons in solution.

The release of so many protons also has an impact on other ions in the solution which contain carbon: in addition to HCO_3, the surface waters of the ocean also contain CO_3. The relative amounts of these two part-molecules depends on the number of free protons in the water. The more protons are present, the less CO_3 there is. The lower the pH value of the ocean becomes, the less carbon is present in the form of CO_3. Should we care about a potential reduction of this chemical in the ocean? Does it make a difference?

The answer is a clear and resounding yes! CO_3 is a necessary "building block" for calcium carbonate and there are very many marine organisms that produce calcium carbonate. These include shellfish, some species of seaweed, starfish, corals, and – perhaps most importantly – tiny organisms like coccolithophorids, pteropods and foraminiferans, which drive the carbonate pump (see Chapter 3) and transport carbon in the form of calcium carbonate from the surface to the bottom waters of the ocean. When the pH value decreases, less CO_3 is available and it becomes more and more difficult for these organisms to make their calcium carbonate, and to maintain it, because calcium carbonate is dissolved under acidic conditions. To imagine the influence of acidic conditions on calcium carbonate in the ocean, one needs only to add vinegar (an acid) to baking soda (sodium bicarbonate). The result is, of course, more extreme than the kinds of changes that we are talking about in the ocean of the immediate future. Nevertheless, the basic underlying chemistry is very much the same in both processes.

As noted above, it is possible to predict the future acidity of the oceans simply on the basis of knowledge of ocean conditions and the atmospheric CO_2 concentrations. From the predicted acidity of the future ocean, it is possible to derive the future chemical conditions for the production and maintenance of calcium carbonate by marine organisms. Such analyses indicate that the acidification of the oceans which is already under way as a result of rising atmospheric CO_2 concentrations is sufficient to have a major biological impact. If the carbon dioxide content of the atmosphere continues to increase unchecked, it is estimated that, by 2065, there will be no regions in the world's oceans where the chemical conditions will be sufficient to support the formation of calcium carbonate by corals.

The biological consequences of ocean acidification are dealt with in the next chapter. For the purposes of this chapter, where we consider changes in the global carbon cycle and the role of the oceans in this cycle, the important message is that it is predicted that ocean acidification will most probably weaken the carbonate pump. Here again, we are reminded of the fact that the different components of the Earth System are interconnected. At first glance, it seems hard to believe that a change in atmospheric CO_2 concentrations should influence coral formation or the amount of carbon being transported from the surface to the bottom of the ocean. However, when we understand the systemic interactions between chemistry, physics and biology in the system, it is easy to see how some things as seemingly unrelated as the release of CO_2 to the atmosphere and corals (or the transport of carbon to the ocean bottom) can be linked. In order to safeguard the future of the ocean, it is important that we respect the ocean as being part of the overall Earth System, and that we strive to understand all the interactions within this system.

Despite the fact that our basic understanding of how the Earth

System functions is still fairly rudimentary, it is sufficient to know that when changes are made to one aspect of the system, this can have an unexpected knock-on effect in a completely different part of the system. The CO_2 ocean acidification story also illustrates that humans are a part of the Earth System and that their activities are sufficient to influence the function of the system. In itself, there is nothing terrible about the fact that human activity can influence the function of the Earth System. Many living creatures influence the Earth's functions. What is important, however, is that our society recognizes this power to change the system and uses this power wisely. We must also understand that one thing that seems to distinguish the way in which human activity influences the function of the Earth System from the way in which other organisms do is that our influence seems to have the capacity to change the system over much shorter timescales than other organisms have done. The following example illustrates why the rate at which a change takes place in a component of the system can be so important.

The rate of change

After being confronted with the concept of a more acidic ocean and the dire predictions concerning the future for organisms which produce calcium carbonate in the ocean, some readers might quite rightly point out that atmospheric CO_2 concentrations have been higher in the history of the Earth with no apparent catastrophic consequences for marine life. This is undoubtedly true; before the evolution of photosynthesis, there was probably about twenty times more carbon dioxide in the air than there is today. Even as relatively recently as a few million years ago, CO_2 levels were mostly significantly higher – and the

climate was warmer – than today. Some will, therefore, undoubtedly argue that the Earth System – including the oceans – must
have mechanisms to cope with a wide range of atmospheric CO_2
concentrations and their influence on the system components. In
fact, the ocean does have a natural mechanism for offsetting the
acidifying effects of increasing CO_2 concentrations.

With the rain of tiny calcium carbonate particles falling to
the bottom of the ocean via the carbonate pump, the bottom
waters of the ocean are rich in carbonate ions. This means that
these layers have the chemical potential to neutralize acid. If we
could mix bottom water to the surface, it would neutralize the
acid formed in the surface waters. An analogy here is that when
our garden soil is too acidic, we add lime to make it less so (the
lime, or calcium oxide, used in our gardens is, by the way, made
by heating limestone (calcium carbonate) which originally came
from the bottom of the ocean!).

Throughout history, this is exactly how the Earth System has
coped with the acidification of the ocean's surface waters resulting
from increases in atmospheric CO_2 concentrations. Turbulences
and ocean currents naturally help to mix up the carbonate-rich
bottom waters of the ocean and the surface waters, where
this process can neutralize the acidification brought about by
increases in the atmospheric CO_2 concentration. However, this
mixing occurs on a timescale of thousands of years. From the ice
cores it can be seen that, prior to human influence on the carbon
cycle, the changes that occurred in atmospheric CO_2 concentration also occurred gradually. In an undisturbed Earth System, the
timescale for the change in atmospheric CO_2 and the timescale
for mixing of bottom water and surface water in the ocean have
similar orders of magnitude. In other words, the natural mixing
processes in the ocean have been sufficient to offset the acidifying
effects of the natural fluctuations in atmospheric CO_2.

Today, the concentration of carbon dioxide in the atmosphere is changing at an unprecedented rate. Instead of changes being recorded over thousands of years as they were in the past, we are now experiencing dramatic changes within the course of decades. The rate of change in atmospheric CO_2 concentration is now occurring on a completely different time scale to the one which governs the mixing processes in the oceans. Thus, the mixing of water from the bottom of the ocean can no longer compensate for the acidification of surface ocean waters.

By now, it should be clear that an understanding of the role of the oceans in the global carbon cycle is crucial for predicting future atmospheric CO_2 concentrations and, thus, future climate conditions. It is not only important to understand how the ocean works and what role it plays in the carbon cycle today, but also how the changes occurring in the ocean may potentially alter the role of the ocean in the global cycle of the future. If, for example, both the biological pump and the carbonate pump in the ocean are weakened due to man-made influences on the Earth System – which is predicted – then the ocean's capacity to take up CO_2 will be reduced. This will mean that atmospheric CO_2 concentrations will increase even more quickly than is presently the case and changes in climate will take effect much faster than currently predicted. It is little wonder that scientists are currently focusing considerable effort on obtaining a better understanding of the present and future ocean's role in the changing global carbon cycle.

Nitrogen

Changes in the carbon cycle in the ocean are, then, important for determining the conditions for life on land. In the case of the nitrogen cycle, the situation is almost reversed. Here, it is the major, man-made changes to the land-based nitrogen cycle which have a bearing on living conditions in the oceans and the release of greenhouse gases from the oceans to the atmosphere. As noted in Chapter 3, in an undisturbed nitrogen cycle, biological nitrogen fixation is the main mechanism by which nitrogen enters into the Earth System. Today, this natural mechanism accounts for the introduction of around 100 Tg nitrogen per year ($1 \, Tg = 10^{12} \, g$). On the other hand, human activities (artificial fertilizers, energy production and mass cultivation of nitrogen fixing plants) introduce in the region of 150 Tg of nitrogen to the Earth System, and it has been projected that the human impact on the nitrogen cycle will increase even further in the future.

Scientists have not yet been able to determine where all of the excess nitrogen introduced by human activities into the Earth System actually ends up. However, it is clear that, although it is initially introduced into the land component of the Earth System, not all of it remains on land. Some of this nitrogen is released to the atmosphere through, for example, combustion processes (including combustion in automobile engines) during which nitrogen oxides are produced, as well as through agriculture (ammonia release) and the release of nitrous oxide (dinitrous monoxide, N_2O) from combustion and biochemical processes. Some of these nitrogen compounds released to the atmosphere are potent greenhouse gases and, therefore, cause concern because of their influence on climate conditions.

In addition, a significant proportion of the nitrogen introduced to the Earth System through human activities on land ends up in the ocean: firstly with the water that flows from the land into the sea (either as untreated waste water or from so-called diffuse sources such as runoff from agricultural land) and, secondly, from the air. The latter occurs both in the form of dry particles and in the form of precipitation which "washes" some of the nitrogen out of the atmosphere and into the ocean.

As noted above, it can be assumed that nitrogen availability determines the amount of phytoplankton photosynthesis which takes place in most regions of the ocean. Therefore, the introduction of this element into marine systems will normally result in an increase in phytoplankton activity – particularly in coastal regions, where there is also anthropogenic phosphorus enrichment of marine waters. While the growth and photosynthesis of most phytoplankton communities are initially limited by nitrogen availability, any limitation is canceled out by the introduction of additional quantities of nitrogen; as a consequence, the availability of phosphorus becomes the new deciding factor. Thus, when nitrogen and phosphorus are added together, any potential limitation on phytoplankton photosynthesis by both of these nutrients is removed. Remember that photosynthesis is the process whereby inorganic carbon (CO_2) is converted to organic material (living organisms). Consequently, an increase in phytoplankton photosynthesis results in an increased production of organic carbon in the system in which the photosynthesis is taking place. This process is called eutrophication (over-fertilization).

At first glance, eutrophication of an ocean system might appear to be a good thing: the increased capture of CO_2 via phytoplankton photosynthesis might be predicted to reduce the amount of CO_2 in the atmosphere, and the introduction of more organic material might be predicted to make more food available in the food chain and, thus, to provide the basis for the production of more fish.

However, things are not always as simple and straightforward as they seem at first glance. It is true that increased rates of photosynthesis increase the amount of CO_2 taken up from the atmosphere by the ocean. However, eutrophication is a coastal phenomenon and, near the coasts, the oceans are shallow. This means that the carbon incorporated into organic material via photosynthesis cannot be transported to the deep ocean layers that are out of contact with the atmosphere for thousands of years. In the surface water, the organic material is broken down again, and the carbon contained in it is released again. The responsibility for this lies with either the metabolism of the phytoplankton themselves or the organisms which eat or decompose them. The additional CO_2 fixed as a result of the stimulation of photosynthesis by nitrogen/phosphorus enrichment of the ocean only remains in the ocean for a short time before it is, again, released to the atmosphere; thus, the net effect is that there is no removal of CO_2 from the atmosphere.

With respect to a possible stimulation of the food chain and an increase in, for example, fisheries as a result of eutrophication, the situation is a little more complicated. It is true that production at the higher levels of some food chains is often limited by the available amount of phytoplankton. In such cases, an increase in phytoplankton may result in a stimulation of the food chain. However, there are many other factors (for example, the temperature) which can limit production in marine food chains. Accordingly, the bulk of the additional organic material produced in response to nutrient enrichment does not get eaten in the water column but, instead, sinks to the floor of the ocean as sediment. Once there, it gets decomposed by bacteria and other organisms. This decomposition process requires oxygen. This means that a very common effect of a stimulation of phytoplankton photosynthesis is a reduction of oxygen in the sediment and bottom waters. Sometimes this reduction is so extreme that there is no longer any oxygen at all present. A low oxygen concentration (hypoxia) or lack of oxygen (anoxia) can lead to mass mortalities of bottom-dwelling organisms and fish. However, in terms of changes in global element cycles, what is more important is that the rates of different chemical reactions involving these elements change with changing oxygen availability.

For example, the cycles of nitrogen, phosphorus, carbon and sulfur are all closely linked to oxygen availability. The oceans are the Earth's most important arena for so-called denitrification, a bacterial process by which N_2 is released to the atmosphere. This process is extremely sensitive to oxygen availability. In addition, the ocean is an important source of nitrous oxide (N_2O); it is estimated that approximately 15% of global emissions of this gas may originate from the oceans. The oxygen depletion resulting from eutrophication has been shown to increase the ocean's N_2O emissions in some regions. Likewise, methane production and release from the ocean is related to local oxygen conditions.

As yet, no one knows whether the increased flow of gases into the atmosphere – which results from changes in oxygen availability in coastal waters and sediments stemming from eutrophication – are quantitatively important on a global scale. However, not least in light of the fact that both methane and nitrous oxide are potent greenhouse gases, this question is currently the focus of much research activity. The fact that artificial fertilizers used on land have, at least theoretically, the very real potential to contribute to global warming by stimulating photosynthesis in the ocean, changing chemical conditions at the bottom of the ocean and, thereby, increasing the release of greenhouse gases into the atmosphere, reminds us once again that the Earth System is one that is complicated and tightly interwoven, where a change in one part of the system can trigger unexpected responses elsewhere.

Sulfur

The final global element cycle we will consider here is the sulfur cycle. As with both the carbon cycle and the nitrogen cycle, the amount of this element being actively turned over in the Earth System has increased dramatically as a result of human activities. Sulfur is an important component of the atmosphere. Before the industrial revolution, sulfur was released to the atmosphere as a result of natural physical processes (i.e. via volcanic eruptions which release sulfur dioxide, SO_2) and biogenic processes (i.e. biomass burning and emissions by soils and plants). Today, however, around 75% of all sulfur emissions are caused by human activity. The element plays a role in climate control, as it is involved in the formation and chemistry of clouds and it is the element which is responsible for "acid rain," i.e. precipitation with a reduced pH value. Until we started to reduce the emissions of sulfur through filters in power stations, this acid rain caused acidification of fresh water and forests.

Sulfur is released to the atmosphere in a number of forms. The most important compounds from the ocean are dimethylsulfide (DMS) and carbon disulfide (CS_2). In terms of quantity, the oceans are the most important natural source of sulfur today, supplying around 15% of the total sulfur emissions into the atmosphere. At present, we do not know enough about the absolute quantities of sulfur contained in the oceans or about the release of sulfur from the oceans. However, there is good reason to believe that the kinds of physical changes predicted for the future ocean (warmer temperatures and increased water column stratification) will favor phytoplankton species which release sulfur (see Chapter 3). We can, therefore, assume that the role of the oceans in the global sulfur cycle will become even greater in the future.

Summary

We have looked in some detail at three global element cycles and the role that the ocean plays in these cycles. These three cycles are very different in many respects. In the case of carbon, the anthropogenic changes in the concentration of CO_2 in the atmosphere have had the most profound effect in terms of disturbing the global cycle but it is a little-appreciated fact that it is reactions which take place in the oceans which are actually controlling the concentration of CO_2 in the atmosphere. In the case of nitrogen, anthropogenic perturbation of the land-based component of the global cycle has had the most dramatic impact. However, these land-based changes are, in turn, causing changes in both the ocean and the atmosphere. In the case of sulfur, anthropogenic release of this element to the atmosphere has had the most dramatic impact on the global cycle. This sulfur enrichment of the atmosphere has serious implications for conditions on land through the production of acid rain. In addition, the increase in sulfur compounds in the atmosphere may have climate implications in that they react with particles in the atmosphere and can, thus, alter the infrared radiation properties of the atmosphere; this means that they may actually help to mitigate the effects of global warming.

With all three of these element cycles, human activities have dramatically altered the magnitude of fluctuations in the system. Consequently, these cycles clearly demonstrate the ability of our species to alter the function of the Earth System. In addition, looking at all three elements helps us to understand how complicated and closely interlinked the functions of the Earth System are. It is absolutely vital to understand the workings of this system in order to be able to predict how human activities will impact upon it.

There is, however, perhaps another reason – possibly the most important reason of all – why it is so important to understand in detail how the Earth System works. The man-made changes we have described here in these three global element cycles are all changes that were brought about inadvertently. Nobody considered the fact that an obvious consequence of the Industrial Revolution, i.e. the increased release of CO_2 to the atmosphere, could ultimately lead to climate change or acidification of the ocean. Even at the time of the agricultural "green revolution," which occurred long after onset of the Industrial Revolution following the invention of artificial fertilizers, no one considered the fact that the chemistry and biology of the oceans and the atmosphere could be altered as a result. Only now are we beginning to understand how the Earth System works, and how the well-intentioned actions of our species over the past two centuries have altered this system.

This understanding is slowly enabling us to alter global element cycles deliberately, rather than inadvertently. Already, proposals are appearing in prestigious scientific journals as to how global elemental cycles might be deliberately manipulated in order to combat the predicted effects of climate change. Such proposals include, for example, the deliberate release of certain sulfur compounds into the atmosphere in an attempt to alter its radiative properties and, thus, reduce the rate of global warming, and the deliberate fertilization of the open ocean in an attempt to increase biological uptake of CO_2 from the atmosphere and to stimulate the biological pump which transports carbon from the surface to deep ocean waters, and to thus promote the sequestration of CO_2 in the ocean sediments.

We believe that, given the state of our current limited understanding of the workings of the Earth System, it is far too early to grasp all of the potential consequences of such measures.

Nevertheless, it would be a mistake not to acknowledge the fact that our species has, or will soon have, the power to deliberately geotechnically manipulate global element cycles. Undoubtedly, the day will come – probably in the not-too-distant future – when the global community will need to seriously discuss whether and for what purposes such drastic actions should be taken. Deliberate geotechnical manipulation of element cycling is not something that should be done lightly. Indeed, it perhaps never should be undertaken at all. Nevertheless, the fact remains that humans have inadvertently altered global elemental cycles to such an extent that it is impossible not to see the unexpected and dramatic responses in the workings of the Earth System. It is not immediately clear whether a reduction of the man-made disturbances (e.g. a reduction in CO_2 emissions) will, on their own, be sufficient to prevent some of the unexpected and undesirable responses to our activities that we are beginning to see.

6 Changes to Life in the Ocean

We use the terms "life in the ocean" or "ocean biology" to describe the total sum of all plants and animals in the ocean. It has become popular in recent years to refer to the combination of different organisms living in any given habitat as the "biodiversity" of that habitat. If we want to examine changes in ocean biology, we must therefore start with changes in the biodiversity of the ocean. There is another important point here: many people believe that human influence on the ocean environment and the biology of the ocean started with pollution and the discharge of waste products from our society into the ocean (see Chapter 7). However, even the earliest human interactions with ocean biology resulted in changes in its biodiversity. Just think of the geographic names like "Turtle Island" or "Walrus Bay;" it is obvious that these areas have been named after the large marine animals which dwelled there and could be hunted – but such animals are now either completely absent or merely occasional visitors.

In a seminal paper from 2001*, the historical relationship between human hunter societies and ocean biology was examined, and the importance of this relationship for the function of ocean ecosystems was established. The study came to the clear

---

* Jackson, J. et al. 2001. 'Historical overfishing and the recent collapse of coastal ecosystems'. *Science*. 293:629–636.

conclusion that human impact on marine ecosystems began far earlier than is generally recognized.

Against the background of this long-standing interaction between humans and the oceans, we will first consider the impact of human activity on biodiversity, before then considering the consequences of modern society using the oceans as a general dumping ground for waste (Chapter 7). However, before dealing with the specific changes in ocean biology and biodiversity along with the causes for these changes, it is worthwhile considering the general concept of biodiversity and examining just what it means for the different components of the Earth System.

The importance of biodiversity

Political and public focus was directed towards biodiversity by the Rio Earth Summit in 1992, where 150 world leaders signed the Convention on Biodiversity (www.biodiv.org), which has the overall aim of ensuring the preservation of biodiversity on Earth. More specifically, one of the stated goals of the Convention is "to achieve by 2010 a significant reduction of the current rate of biodiversity loss at the global, regional and national level as a contribution to poverty alleviation and to the benefit of all life on earth." Accordingly, there is a political understanding that the animals and plants on Earth are important and should be protected, not only for their own sake, but also for the sake of the further development of human society. It is also clear that species are currently disappearing from the face of the Earth at an alarming rate and that all or most of these species losses are related to the destruction of their habitats as a result of human activities.

During the course of the Earth's history, there have been a

number of occasions at which mass extinction of species has occurred. It is thought that this was probably due to dramatic changes in the physical environment. However, the current mass extinction event appears to be the first in the history of the planet which is being caused by a single species (our species!).

Despite clear indications of this glaring loss in biodiversity and the noble intentions of the Convention on Biodiversity, it is difficult to establish a stringent framework to combat the loss. One of the reasons for this is that the composition of the animal and plant communities in a given region constantly changes due to natural fluctuations in climate and environmental changes, in addition to which, over long timescales, some species will always disappear while new ones appear. Therefore, when changes occur in the distribution of species, it can be difficult to ascertain the exact cause for that change and, in particular, it is difficult to determine the contribution made by human activities. It is just as difficult to identify potential countermeasures which could prevent further loss of species. This does not make it easy to set clear targets or develop mechanisms which would allow the goals identified in the Convention on Biodiversity to be attained. Neverthelesss, the intentions are clear enough: our society recognizes that a current mass extinction of the Earth's living organisms is in progress and expresses a political desire to reduce species loss due to human activities. This applies to the biodiversity of the entire Earth. However, conserving biodiversity in the ocean is a particularly difficult challenge, as we understand so little about life in the ocean (see Chapter 2).

Any efforts to protect nature in the ocean face a special problem, in that so many of the species which dwell in the ocean are too small to be seen by the naked eye. Ask almost anyone which forms of marine life should be protected with the greatest urgency, and they will, almost certainly, name the largest animals first and then move down in size: whales, other marine mammals and, finally, fish. A few might argue that some seabed-dwelling animals such as starfish, snails or sea urchins are worthy of protection – but little concern would be expressed for organisms that are smaller. Nevertheless, as we saw in Chapter 3, it is the very smallest of organisms in the ocean that have the greatest importance for our environment. Unfortunately, there is little appreciation for the fact that life in the oceans is important for human societies in many different ways – and not just because it provides us with food in the form of fish!

Consequently, the best solution in terms of protecting nature in the ocean is not to protect individual species but to protect and conserve as many different marine habitats as possible with the aid of Marine Protected Areas (MPA).

Although these areas will not be able to arrest climate change and acidification, they will nevertheless protect ecosystems against numerous other interventions and offer a retreat for species which are under threat due to overfishing. This type of protection area can, therefore, significantly enhance the resilience of marine ecosystems, particularly if they are widened to form a comprehensive and ecologically representative network of protection areas. In a special report published in 2006, the German Advisory Council on Global Change (WBGU) proposed that 20 to 30% of the world's oceans should be protected in this manner.

Another factor which confounds the political intention of conserving biodiversity is that it is still not entirely clear exactly what biodiversity means for the functioning of a given ecosystem. Should we worry about the loss of a single species? What is the "value" of that species for us? How important is it for an ecosystem to have several different organisms which all carry out the same fundamental function? Are all species equally important?

And, if it is not possible to protect all species, are there any that play a more pivotal role in the functioning of an ecosystem than others? These are questions that the scientific community is currently grappling with.

Some clear examples are emerging which underline how important biodiversity is for marine ecosystems. For example, coral reef ecologists working in Discovery Bay off Jamaica were taken by surprise in the 1980s when the corals there became smothered in algal growth during the course of just a very few years. The immediate cause appeared to be an epidemic which decimated the dominant native sea urchin (*Diadema antillarum*) population. This sea urchin feeds on organisms which dwell on the surface of corals. In this way, it frees the corals – among other things – from the algae, by preventing it from becoming established and suffocating the corals. When the epidemic decimated the sea urchin population, there was nothing to stop the algae from establishing a foothold, and then smothering the corals.

At first glance, this change in species distribution and, therefore, the function of this marine system might easily be assumed to be an act of nature and not something which was influenced by human activity. However, a more thorough analysis of the collapse of the sea urchin population suggests that it was, indeed, human activity that led to this functional change in the ecosystem. Prior to the outbreak of the epidemic, the sea urchin population had risen dramatically. In fact, the epidemic itself was probably stimulated by a high population density and the resulting close contact between individual sea urchins. The cause of this increase in the sea urchin population was, most probably, twofold: firstly, there was a reduction in the numbers of predators on the sea urchins, and this coincided with an increased availability of food. Both factors were probably the result of intensive fishing in the coral reef in the period preceding the explosion in the sea urchin population.

Some of the fish on the reef feed on the sea urchins. As a result, they exert predation pressure and control on the numbers of urchins present. Fishing on the reef reduced the predation pressure on the sea urchins by removing the predators that fed upon them. Like the sea urchins, other fish on the reef feed upon the small organisms which live on the surface of the corals. This means that these species are in competition with the sea urchins for food. As the numbers of these fish also decreased, there was more food available for the sea urchins. With the reduction in predation pressure on the urchins and the increased availability of food, the urchin population grew more or less unchecked until it reached a density where the disease could spread rapidly and this caused a mass mortality which resulted in a severe reduction in the size of the population. Prior to the intensive fishing on the reef, even after a mass mortality among the sea urchins, there would still have been other organisms (fish) which would have "cleaned" the surface of the corals while feeding. Consequently, in addition to setting the scene for an explosion in the sea urchin population, the intensive fishing on the reef also intervened into the coral reef ecosystem and stopped it from being able to prevent the corals from being overgrown by algae.

Similar examples are now known from a whole range of marine ecosystems which all show that it is precisely the interactions between the organisms present which maintain the ecosystem in its current state. An example such as the one presented here for coral reefs in the Caribbean illustrates how important it can be to have more than one species capable of fulfilling specific functions if the ecosystem is to retain an overall level of resilience. Finally, the example given here also underlines once again the importance of predators for the structuring of marine ecosystems, while also emphasizing the fact that the components this type of system are interlinked in complicated and unexpected ways.

In recent years, more and more examples of the type described above which emphasize the importance of biodiversity for ecosystems have been identified. Not surprisingly, most of these involve the large organisms which form part of the systems – not only can they be observed with the naked eye, but changes in their abundance immediately become obvious. In some cases, analyses have shown that changes in the interactions between the larger organisms in an ecosystem have indirect effects on the components of the ecosystem which are dominated by microscopic organisms. For example, the removal of mussels, which filter the water in order to take up food, causes an increase in the phytoplankton population, which in turn leads to algal blooms and a reduction in the oxygen content and water quality. In addition, some studies have focused directly on the importance of biodiversity of organisms which do not immediately catch the eye (for example, worms in the ocean sediment). These studies also offer indications that biodiversity increases both the total productivity and the resilience of an ecosystem in the face of disturbances.

Of course, not all studies arrive at the same results in terms of biodiversity and the functioning of ecosystems. Nevertheless, a sufficient number of studies have now been conducted to paint a general picture of the overall role of biodiversity. Recently, several studies on marine biodiversity have been published and they all draw the conclusion that ecosystem productivity and resilience can often be linked to biodiversity. The scientific community is now gradually starting to document the general importance of combating species loss – not simply for the sake of the threatened organisms themselves, but also for the functioning of ecosystems and, ultimately, for the preservation of the services that ecosystems provide to both human societies and the Earth System as a whole.

Despite this emerging consensus, it is still not clear whether particular species or groups of species are more important than others for ecosystems and, if so, how these species or groups can be identified and protected. Research into the significance of bio-diversity for the functioning of ecosystems and, therefore, for the capacity of ecosystems to provide services in the Earth System is on-going. This research is urgently required if we are to offer advice to political decision makers about how best to achieve the goals of the Convention on Biological Diversity.

The effects of fishing

Fishing is the most obvious way in which humans interact with ocean biology, and it is fishing – alongside the hunting of even large marine mammals – that has had the first human impact on ocean biodiversity. Today, something on the order of 100 million tons of human food in the form of fish are taken from the ocean every year – either by fishing wild stocks or from aquaculture. In addition to the fish caught and used directly as food for human consumption, another approximately 20 million tons is caught for industrial purposes (e.g. for fish meal used as food additives, in agriculture or in aquaculture). Fishing has increased dramatically in recent decades. At the beginning of the 1950s, under 10% of fish stocks in the world's oceans were fully fished. Today, around 70% of global fish stocks are fully fished, with 20% of these stocks being overfished to a point which can no longer be considered to be sustainable. In other words, it is believed that fishing cannot continue at the current level in these regions without eventually destroying

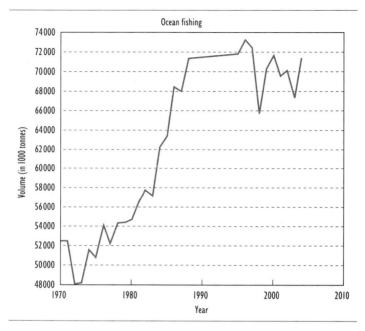

Figure 6.1 The catches of wild fish have remained static for several years

the fish stocks altogether. There seems little reason to believe that it would be possible to take greater quantities of wild fish from the sea than we already catch today and the amount of fish caught has, indeed, stagnated in recent years (see Fig. 6.1). Accordingly, the increases in yield recently reported by the Food and Agriculture Organization (FAO) all stem from an increase in aquaculture.

We often hear in the news that fishermen and biologists disagree about the current state of fish stocks, with fishermen claiming that there are still plenty of fish and that the biologists who argue that stocks are threatened simply don't know how to fish, or that they look for fish in all the wrong places! To make sense of this conflict, it is worthwhile considering how biologists assess fish stocks and it is also important to understand how and why their fishing strategies differ from those of the fishermen who make a living by catching as many fish as possible.

The goal of biologists is not to catch as many fish as possible. Their goal is to determine how many specimens are at a given spot in the ocean this year so that the current numbers can be compared to past data, i.e. data from last year, the year before that or twenty or more years ago. In order to make this type of comparison, it is important that biologists use the same equipment and methods as those employed when the time series was started. Obviously, if the biologists change to more effective and more modern equipment, more fish will be caught and it will appear that there are more fish in the ocean now than was the case in earlier years. This is why biologists use "old-fashioned" equipment which is known to be less effective than the modern equipment used by commercial fishers.

Another criticism directed at biologists by fishermen is that the biologists fish in places where it is known there are no fish. On the face of it, this criticism seems fair. However, biologists do this on purpose. Fish migrate around during the course of the year and, when populations shrink, they steadily occupy less of the marine landscape as a whole. For biologists, it is important to gain a picture of the absolute number of fish in the entire area. To do this, they employ a "grid" of fixed positions at which samples are taken every year. It may well be known that there are no or only a few fish at a given fishing location but, if fish have been caught in this location in the past, then knowing that there are no fish today is important information for the biologist. Of course, fishermen would never fish in a location where they know that there are no fish. Therefore, the behavior of the biologist can be hard for fishermen to understand.

What the biologists are trying to do is to estimate the number of female fish in a given population. Why female fish? Well, these are of course the fish on which the future of the stock depends. Up until a certain point, increasing the number of female fish will also increase the number of young fish that can grow up to be a part of the fishable population. We call the number of young fish that grow to a size at which they can be fished "recruits."

However, there comes a point when increased numbers of female fish do not equate to an increased supply of recruits into the fishable population. This is because when there are very many mothers and, therefore, very many baby fish, there is not enough food for all of the babies. In addition, when there are large numbers of young, they actually eat one another in some cases (remember how important predation is for structuring eco-systems in the ocean!). Consequently, when there are very many baby fish, a large number of them starve or are eaten before they are large enough to be fished.

The goal of fisheries management is to try and ensure that the number of female fish remains as close as possible to the number at which the maximum number of recruits is produced. This means that the numbers of mother fish are maintained at a level where their reproduction leads to the maximum possible number of young fish joining the fishable population. In order to be sustainable, fisheries should be satisfied with the number of mother fish whose presence does not lead to an increase in the size of the stock that is fishable in the future.

Taking cod in the North Sea as an example, all available data indicate that the number of young fish which forms the future stock increases until the number of mother fish reaches something around 150,000 t. In an ideal world, fishing pressure should be regulated so that the stocks of mother fish remain at approximately this level. However, natural fluctuations in stock size and the economic realities of the fishing industry dictate that it will never be possible to exactly maintain this level. Therefore, biologists have "arbitrarily" developed a rule of thumb according to which the stocks of mother fish should not be allowed to fall below half the amount which yields the greatest number of recruits. In the case of the North Sea, this means that biologists advise that the mother stock should not be allowed to fall below about 70,000 t. Nevertheless, current stocks of cod mother fish are estimated to be only around 50,000 t. This explains why biologists have advocated that cod fishery should be temporarily stopped in the North Sea altogether.

However, despite the biologists' recommendations, for obvious economic reasons politicians have chosen not to suspend the fishing of cod in the North Sea but to postpone the "recovery program" for this stock. It is interesting that this political decision to "postpone" the recovery plan is based on the assumption that, if a fish stock has been overfished down to very low numbers, it will return to its previously recorded numbers when the fishing pressure is removed. There is, however, no guarantee that this will be the case. One of the most dramatic illustrations of this fact comes from the cod population off the eastern coast of Canada, i.e. around Newfoundland.

This population was one of the attractions held by the New World for early European explorers and settlers, and their diaries report prolific catches, the like of which they had never experienced before. Ever since humans have lived in this region, the stocks have been a mainstay of the economy. However, by the early 1990s, stocks had dwindled to such low numbers that a total ban on cod fishing was imposed in 1992. Over fifteen years later, there is still no sign that the stocks are recovering. No one knows for sure why the numbers are not improving. However, other species (i.e. lobsters) are now more abundant in the region than they were during the times of high cod stocks.

The massive increase in other species may be explained by the fact that the overfishing of cod reduced the pressures upon these other populations. With the removal of the cod as a predator, more of the juvenile lobsters survive and the stock of lobsters becomes larger. Here, again, we are reminded of the fact that predation is a very important structuring factor in marine ecosystems. It is tempting to suggest that other species may have moved in and filled the niches in the ecosystem which were once occupied by cod. The fact that these niches are now no longer free makes it difficult for the cod to return.

A current consensus is emerging within the scientific community that there may be more than one natural state for an ecosystem. In other words, there is no natural law which states that cod must be a part of a "healthy" North Atlantic ecosystem. Even without the cod, the ecosystem can be just as natural and "healthy," provided other species fill the gap created by the absence of cod and fulfill the same ecological functions as cod. Moving from one natural state to another is referred to as a regime shift. Sometimes it is nature itself which brings about these changes, for example as a consequence of changes in climatic conditions. However, more and more indicators suggest that regime shifts can also be brought about through human intervention, for example by overfishing. In order to develop sustainable fisheries, it is important to take into account the possibility that overfishing can change the state of the ecosystem. The assumption that there is a linear relationship between the size of a commercially-important stock such as cod and the intensity with which the fish is harvested does not necessarily hold true. Instead, there can be a critical limit at which the ecosystem "tips over." It is, therefore, both wrong and dangerous to regulate fishing quotas on the basis of this assumption.

Obviously, fisheries potentially affect the abundance of their target species and the biodiversity of the ocean. In some cases where stocks are heavily fished, as in the example of cod in the North Sea, around 70% or more of the biomass of the species is fished out of the ocean – every year! At least until relatively recently, fisheries management has only been concerned with the size of the target stock and an estimation of the fishing pressure that the stock can tolerate. Until the 1990s, there was little concern for non-target species or the possible consequences of fishing on the structure of and interactions in the ecosystem. In 1998, however, a group of researchers analyzed FAO catch statistics and hypothesized that fisheries have changed the structure of ecosystems in such a manner that the larger fish have essentially disappeared from all of the world's oceans. Their reasoning was based on the observation that, according to FAO data, the size of the fish being caught has been getting smaller and smaller in recent years compared to previous decades (D. Pauly et al. 1998). Needless to say, this study attracted much attention (and fierce debate) and is still a focus of much interest in the scientific community.

Fisheries' biologists were largely reluctant to accept the conclusion that fishing alone is sufficient to destroy ecosystems and they pointed out (quite rightly) that the amounts of fish caught depend on the behavior of fishers, which in turn is governed by the potential market for the fish that they catch. During recent decades, a market has developed for industrial fisheries, i.e. fisheries that target small fish such as sand eels in the North Sea. Fishes caught in industrial fisheries are not sold directly to the consumer but used in the production of fish oil and meal. This industry has, therefore, created a market for smaller fish which could, in theory at least, have caused the changes in the catch data recorded in the FAO statistics. This means that the analysis of commercial catch data alone will never be sufficient to allow changes in ecosystem structures to be identified with any certainty.

Nevertheless, the fact that the question was raised at all and the suggestion was made that there may now be fewer large fish in the world ocean than a few decades ago caused other researchers to examine this problem using different methods. As a result, it has indeed emerged that for a number of different marine regions (including the North Sea), it can be demonstrated that there are fewer large fish and more small fish today than 30–40 years ago. Demonstrating that this change has occurred does not in itself, of course, necessarily identify fishing as the cause of the change. However, given the fact that most fisheries focus their efforts on the large fish and that fishing removes up to over 70% of some species in heavily fished areas in any given year, fisheries are certainly an obvious candidate for having caused this change in ecosystem structure. When considering the potential for fisheries to change the structure of marine ecosystems, it is also worth remembering that predation is seen as a dominant force in the structuring of marine ecosystems and that fishing is the ultimate form of predation.

In addition to potentially influencing the structure of marine food chains by changing the relative distribution of large and small fish present in the sea, it is now also recognized that fishing can exert a genetic pressure on fish populations and may therefore alter the gene pool of certain stocks. There are several mechanisms by which this may occur: intensive fishing removes the larger fish from the population. One consequence of this is a selection pressure which favors individual fish which become sexually mature the earliest (because those which mature later are fished out of the sea before they have had a chance to reproduce). Regionally focused fishing pressure can eliminate sub-populations of fish, for example. No one knows what the long-term consequences (if indeed there are any) of the genetic selection pressure exerted on fish stocks are, but the fact that this selection appears to take place reminds us once again that human activities are a major force in the Earth System, a force that must be taken into account when considering the function of the system.

Bycatch and waste

Of course, fishing also affects other organisms than just the target fish stocks. Bottom trawl nets do not specifically target fish which are intended to be caught. In some intensively fished regions, the seabed is turned over or "ploughed" several times per year. It goes without saying that this destroys the more fragile organisms living there and the frequent disturbance of the seabed means that the bottom fauna has to re-establish itself repeatedly. Accordingly, the bottom fauna in such areas is dominated by young and fast-growing species.

Most of the non-target organisms caught during the fishing process (and this includes both bottom animals and non-target fish caught in the water column) are simply thrown back into the sea. At first glance, this might be regarded as being a good thing for life in the ocean. However, being caught in a trawl net is a violent process and most of the animals that are returned as "discards" to the sea after having been caught in fish trawls are either already dead or die upon their return. The numbers of discards from some fisheries is astounding and can add up to more than the amount of the target species caught. In the North Sea, it is estimated that 22% of the fish and bottom invertebrates caught every year in fisheries never arrive on land but are thrown back into the sea as waste or discards.

Some of this waste (about 63,000 t) consists of offal from the processing of fish catches on board, but about ten times that amount consists of whole fish. In addition, about 15,000 t of sharks, skates and rays and 150,000 t of bottom-dwelling (benthic) invertebrates are caught and thrown back as discards. All this adds up to tremendous quantities of biological material that is discarded in the form of fish and other animals from fisheries in the North Sea – an amount which is the equivalent of about 4% of the total fish biomass in the North Sea. Looking at this amount of material, it is also interesting to ask how much food it represents in the food chain, and where in the food chain it ends up after having made a trip up onto the deck of a fishing boat.

Birds are clearly the biggest beneficiaries of the "free lunch" provided by these discards and it is estimated that the energy demands of almost six million birds are met by fishing waste and discards. It is documented that there has been a huge increase in the numbers of birds (especially gulls and related species) in the North Sea over the past century and it is most probable that this increase is largely a response to the development of large-scale fisheries in the same period. Many environmental organizations are now calling for a stop to the practice of large-scale discarding of fishing waste and there are many good arguments for such a stop. However, it should also be borne in mind that such a stop would inevitably lead to a reduction in the food available for the bird population and to the mass starvation and die-off of birds in the North Sea area.

The so-called bycatch can also affect the stock size of the species caught. However, it is difficult to correctly assess this potential effect because of a lack of availability of good data which can be used to understand changes through time in the abundance and distribution of these species. Fisheries management has been practiced since the middle of the last century in most developed countries and, in this context, data have been collected on the abundance and distribution of commercially important fish stocks. With the aid of these numbers, we can follow how the sizes of commercially interesting stocks have developed over time. Unfortunately though, no such data have been collected on the species which are not of any commercial interest. As a result, the long-term impact of fisheries on many species that are frequently caught as bycatch is unknown. Nevertheless, the abundance of fish such as skates, rays and sharks is believed to have been severely reduced in some regions of the world's oceans as a result of fishing. In addition, some of the species which dwell at the bottom of the ocean have probably suffered but, owing to lack of data on bottom communities in the open ocean, the extent to which fisheries have impacted these organisms will probably never be known.

As was explained in Chapter 5, the changes taking place in the Earth System relate to much more than just climate – and one of the major global changes during the past half-century has been the global intensification of fishing. Fishing is important, as it provides an important source of food for our own species. In some regions of the world, fisheries provide the major or even sole source of protein intake for many people. However, for the biology and ecology of the ocean itself, fisheries have major consequences and have already brought about some major changes. Fishing practices will have to change, and the focus of fisheries management will need to shift so that it takes into consideration not only the state of the target species, but also the influence of fisheries on the functioning of the ocean as a whole if we are to ensure that future generations will still be able to harvest the oceans for their own benefit. Although fishing is probably the human activity which has most directly affected ocean biology until now, there are a number of other global changes caused by human activity which, directly or indirectly, already influence ocean biology now or will come to do so in the future. Let us now look at some of these.

Nutrient enrichment

We saw in Chapter 5 that the global nitrogen cycle has been dramatically changed – not least of which through the development of artificial fertilizers – and that much of the nitrogen released on land ultimately finds its way into coastal waters. This stimulates phytoplankton photosynthesis – which can lead to an increased deposition of organic material and oxygen depletion in bottom waters – and also influences the exchange of gas between the ocean and the atmosphere. In addition, the increased transport of nitrogen to coastal waters also influences ocean organisms.

The most obvious change this nutrient enrichment brings about is an increase in the phytoplankton biomass. The fact that there is more phytoplankton in the water column means that light cannot penetrate as deeply into the water as before the nutrient enrichment. Put differently, this means that less light reaches the bottom – and the plants living on the bottom cannot survive. As a result, the small phytoplankton living in the water column become the dominant plants instead of larger plants that live on the bottom. This is one of the first reactions to nutrient enrichment and is, in fact, an example of a "regime shift," where the system moves from one state (in which large bottom plants dominate) to another (in which small phytoplankton in the water column dominate).

Interestingly, when the nutrient enrichment is stopped, the system does not automatically revert back to the original state. With increasing nutrient input, the water becomes less and less clear thanks to the increasing phytoplankton biomass; but when the nutrient enrichment is reduced, the process does not reverse. In other words, the system is now in a new state dominated by phytoplankton.

This is another example which demonstrates that marine systems do not necessarily respond linearly to change (for example, nutrient enrichment or overfishing). An increase in nutrient input leads to the loss of bottom plants but a decrease does not automatically lead to the return of these organisms. Similarly, as has already been discussed, an increase in fishing pressure can significantly reduce the stock size. However, a decrease in fishing pressure does not necessarily lead to an increase in stock size of the target species. It is absolutely vital that we remember this if we are ever to achieve a sustainable use of the ocean.

Marine ecosystems are robust and can tolerate a lot of pressure, for example from fishing or nutrient enrichment. However, there are thresholds – and if we push the system beyond one of these thresholds, it may end up developing in a completely different way to which we are accustomed. In terms of ocean biology and management of the ocean, this means two things: firstly, it is essential that we gain a better understanding of how marine systems work, so we can predict where these thresholds may be, and secondly, in terms of ocean management, it is crucial that we avoid getting close to these thresholds.

In addition to changing the predominant plant form from benthic (i.e. bottom-living) to pelagic (i.e. living in the water column), nutrient enrichment changes the relative abundance of organisms in the different compartments of the food chain.

Phytoplankton biomass increases. To a certain degree, this means more food for the next level in the food chain (zooplankton). Not all of the phytoplankton is eaten, however, and this results in an accumulation of phytoplankton – a so-called "algal bloom." These algal blooms are often harmful to humans (both commercially and/or in terms of public health) – particularly in cases where the phytoplankton are toxic (see Chapter 3). The oxygen depletion resulting from decaying phytoplankton which fall to the ocean floor makes conditions there unsuitable for numerous other organisms living on or near the bottom, and many of these organisms disappear. Consequently, the implications of nutrient enrichment for biodiversity – at least for the organisms which are large enough for us to see with the naked eye – are well known (and have been observed in coastal waters all around the world).

Something which is often largely ignored is the impact of nutrient enrichment on the biodiversity of the tiny phytoplankton themselves. We have discovered that phytoplankton as a group become more abundant after nutrient enrichment but, until recently, we have either assumed that all members of the phytoplankton community are stimulated equally, or that possible changes in the community do not make a difference to the structure of the food chain. It is only now that scientists are beginning to realize that the most common forms of anthropogenic nutrient enrichment may, in fact, change the phytoplankton community in such a way that small phytoplankton cells become more dominant than they were prior to nutrient enrichment. How can this be?

In most coastal waters, nitrogen is the dominant anthropogenic nutrient input. This means that the ratio of availability of the essential nutrients nitrogen and phosphorus becomes skewed towards nitrogen in comparison to what is normally found in the ocean. Access to nitrogen is, therefore, not a problem for the phytoplankton. However, the organisms are forced to compete with each other for the now scarce resource, phosphorus. We saw in Chapter 2 that it is an advantage to be a small cell when competing for nutrients, as small cells have a relatively large surface area in relation to their volume. Even if the change in the ecosystem is brought about by an increase in the availability of nutrients (nitrogen) and our traditional understanding of ocean biology tells us that large phytoplankton should dominate under high nutrient availability, the fact that the ratio of available nutrients is now skewed in comparison to the normal conditions means that small phytoplankton may actually come to dominate. While the mechanisms controlling size structure in phytoplankton communities are not yet well understood, available data indicate that smaller cells do dominate in systems experiencing severe eutrophication.

A change from large to small phytoplankton cells leads to less efficient energy transfer in the food chain (see Chapter 2) and this means that the system can become less productive at the higher trophic levels (i.e. at the level of the fish). In other words, because the phytoplankton cells are small, the increase in phytoplankton caused by nutrient enrichment will not necessarily lead to greater food availability for fish.

This example again reminds us of the fact that the Earth System is interconnected in many intricate and unexpected ways. A change in the system as a whole (if for example more atmospheric nitrogen is fixed and introduced into the terrestrial system) can lead to unexpected changes in the function of the system (such as a change in the size distribution of the tiny plants in the ocean which, in turn, can influence fish production). In addition, the example reminds us of course that, even amongst the organisms which are too small for us to see with the naked eye, biodiversity matters for system function.

Rising sea temperatures

Many researchers are currently focusing their efforts on trying
to predict the potential consequences of global warming on life
in the oceans. This is not an easy task for a number of reasons.
Firstly, forecasts of future climate conditions are usually based
on changes in *average* temperature over the period of a year or
season. Of course, no organism on Earth lives at average temperatures. If you have your head in an oven and your feet in a freezer,
you may have a perfectly comfortable average temperature.
However, the extreme temperatures at either end of your body
will undoubtedly cause you discomfort. The same applies to all
organisms (whether on land or in the ocean – including humans!)
when it comes to survival in a changing climate regime.

Predictions about the potential effects of warming on marine
organisms are also made more difficult by the fact that marine
food chains are complex and precarious. They interlink species
in such a way that it is not enough to understand the temperature
response of the different species in order to be able to predict the
effects of warming on them. At the same time, it is also necessary
to understand the potential effects of climate warming on all of
the organisms upon which all of the life stages of the species in
question are dependent for food.

A good example of this is the tiny copepod, *Calanus finmarchicus*, we met in Chapter 2. The survival of juvenile cod
in the North Sea is dependent upon the availability of this
organism as food. However, changes in the current system
brought about by increasing temperatures and a reduction in
the formation of deep water in the Greenland Sea and the Lab-
rador Sea will influence the life cycle of *Calanus* by altering the
transport of this organism to/from the North Sea to the open
North Atlantic and by potentially reducing the overwintering

habitat (cold deep water in the Faeroe-Shetland Channel) of the species.

In order to predict the influence of a warmer climate on the commercially valuable species of cod, it is therefore clearly not enough simply to examine the temperature tolerance of an adult cod. It is also necessary to understand the effects of increasing temperatures on the food organisms on which the cod depends throughout the different stages of its life.

Another good example of the need to understand interactions in entire ecosystems in order to predict the consequences of climate change for particular species is found at the opposite side of the world. The waters of the Antarctic are known for their abundance of whales and penguins. What effects will higher temperatures have on these organisms? A shift in the temperature of the region of a few degrees would probably have barely any direct consequences for these animals. However, the entire food chain in Antarctic waters – including penguins and many whales – depends upon the availability of tiny shrimp-like animals called "krill." The abundance of krill is, in turn, a function of the extent of the sea ice (because the phytoplankton species on which the krill feed are found in large concentrations just under the ice). Increasing temperatures cause the ice to melt and, as a consequence, there are fewer habitats for the phytoplankton, less food for the krill, fewer krill and, ultimately, less food available for whales and penguins.

There are many examples like this, and they all underline time and time again how important it is to understand the interrelationships within the ocean system (or Earth System) in order to be able to predict the response to change of individual components in the system. Although our understanding of these correlations in the ocean system is still incomplete, we can see that the warmer temperatures recorded in recent years in the world's oceans (see Chapter 4) have had an impact on the geographic distributions of some species. Today, more "warm water species" are found at northerly latitudes than before. In the North Sea, there are numerous examples of warm water fish and other species which have become native in recent years thanks to the higher temperatures and milder winters. One interesting example of this type of fish is the European seabass which, until recently, rarely made its way as far north as the North Sea. Now, however, this fish is actively fished as far north as Norway.

One interesting aspect of the appearance of the European seabass in the North Sea is the fact that it brings a parasite with it. This is a worm which uses shellfish as a host during part of its life cycle; its presence in the shellfish, however, makes the shellfish unable to reproduce. After the appearance of the European seabass as a regular member of the fish community in the North Sea, this parasite has appeared for the first time in shellfish in the Wadden Sea along the Dutch, German and Danish coasts. It is, as yet, unknown what, if any, the ecological effects of the introduction of this parasite will be. This example reminds us again, however, that it is not enough to examine temperature responses of individual organisms in order to predict the consequences of global warming on ocean biology. It comes as no surprise that, all around the world, scientists are concentrating on improving our understanding of the interactions between temperature and ecosystem functions.

Life in the ocean under the effects of acidification

A main focus of Chapter 5 was the fact that the increased CO_2 concentration in the atmosphere is causing acidification of surface waters of the ocean. This is a relatively new finding, and the consequences for ocean biology are still not entirely clear. Nevertheless, it would be remiss of us not to briefly consider the possible consequences of acidification on ocean biology.

As was already mentioned in Chapter 5, organisms which form calcium carbonate will be affected most directly, as a more acidic ocean will dissolve calcium carbonate. Calcium carbonate is produced by a whole host of different marine organisms, ranging from seaweeds to corals and the tiny organisms which rain to the bottom of the ocean and eventually form the basis of chalk cliffs. However, it is believed that not all of these organisms are equally susceptible to acidity changes in the ocean.

This is because two different forms of calcium carbonate are produced by ocean organisms: calcite and aragonite. They differ only in terms of their crystal structure, and each group of calcium carbonate-producing organisms only makes one of the two types. Both forms of calcium carbonate dissolve under acidic conditions, but aragonite is more sensitive to changes in acidity. We, therefore, expect that organisms which produce aragonite will be the first to be affected by the increasing acidity of the ocean. Corals produce aragonite and are, thus, predicted to be particularly sensitive to higher levels of ocean acidification. As already discussed in Chapter 5, it is predicted that, by the second half of this century, there will be no regions in the world's oceans where the chemical conditions will support calcium carbonate production by corals if CO_2 concentrations in the atmosphere continue to rise unchecked.

Pteropods are another aragonite-producing group which is particularly vulnerable to ocean acidification (these are tiny, snail-like organisms living in the water column). This group of organisms is particularly important for food chains at high latitudes (i.e. the ecosystems in the Arctic and Antarctic). In the Ross Sea near Antarctica, for example, these organisms are highly abundant and play an extremely important role in the ecosystem there by transporting carbon (both organic carbon and carbon bound in calcium carbonate) to the bottom. This means that not only do they play an essential part in the food chain, but also in the transport of carbon from surface waters to deeper waters where it is not in direct contact with the atmosphere. However, because of the changes in acidity conditions, it is feared that these organisms will disappear from the ecosystem of the Ross Sea within the next fifty years unless the increase in the atmospheric concentration of CO_2 is slowed or stopped. On the other hand, it is believed that organisms which produce calcite (e.g. mussels, snails, lobsters etc.) react less sensitively to changes in ocean acidity – although that, of course, does not mean that they might not also suffer in the event of extreme acidification.

The dissolution of calcium carbonate and the resulting effects on biodiversity are, however, not the only consequences for ocean biology which are expected as a result of acidification. For example, it is known that water-breathing animals (i.e. those that obtain their oxygen from water rather than from air as we do) react particularly sensitively to the ratio of CO_2 to oxygen in the water. It is not yet known whether changes in this ratio resulting from the rising concentration of CO_2 will be significant enough to influence the ability of water-breathing organisms to extract oxygen from seawater, but the answer to this question is currently being sought by a number of scientists worldwide.

Summary

For the most part, life in the oceans is hidden away from view and we, therefore, tend to ignore it most of the time. Nevertheless, it plays a very important role in shaping our land-based environment. And precisely because we so rarely come into direct contact with nature in the ocean, we tend not to realize that our activities are changing the biology and living conditions in the oceans.

When we harvest animals from the ocean (i.e. through hunting and fishing), this obviously has a direct impact on the target organisms – but also on organisms which are inadvertently caught as bycatch. Similarly, changes in nutrient input to the ocean, global warming, and increases in atmospheric CO_2 concentration – which leads to ocean acidification – are all processes which have an impact on ocean biology today and will continue to do so in the future. If we are to develop a sustainable relationship between our species and the planet we inhabit, it is therefore absolutely crucial that we both recognize the importance of ocean biology for the preservation of the Earth System and acknowledge the fact that man-made influences are momentous enough to alter life in the ocean and thereby its functions in the Earth System.

7 The Ocean as a Waste Receptacle

An enormous part of the Earth is covered by water. In view of our own diminutive size and the small amount of space taken up by each individual on Earth, it has always seemed inconceivable to humans that our own activities could possibly have any influence on the workings of the mighty ocean. However, even in so-called developed countries, the realization that the oceans cannot simply be treated by humanity as a giant garbage dump has only recently become established. Even now, it is still common – and generally permitted – in some countries for everything which is no longer needed or of use to be simply thrown into the ocean. In contrast, most industrial nations have strict regulations which control the direct use of the ocean as a waste dump for litter and industrial waste, and the notion that the ocean should be used as a universal dumping ground is rejected by the majority of the population. But this attitude has only emerged in the last one or two generations.

Looking back in time

When considering the future of the oceans and our relationship with them, some interesting insight can be gained by looking back in time: during the historical development of society, how did an appreciation of the potential for human activities to impact the oceans become established? In the industrial nations, our relationship with the oceans gradually began to become an issue of public concern in the 1950–60s, when it became clear that the process of dumping toxic industrial waste off coastal waters was harmful. This was partly thanks to books written by ecologists and environmental campaigners, who presented scientific findings about the functions of the ocean to a wider audience (e.g. Rachel Carson's *The Sea Around Us*, which was published in 1951) and partly thanks to the publicity concerning the catastrophic consequences of dumping chemical waste. One particularly extreme case which received a great deal of public attention was the Minamata tragedy in Japan. In the 1950s and 1960s, it became increasingly apparent that years of chemical effluent discharge into the coastal waters of an industrial town located some 900 km southwest of Tokyo had made the population of the town seriously ill. Subsequent analysis indicated that, between 1932 and 1968, at least 27 tons of mercury compounds had been dumped into the bay and that the resulting "Minamata disease" was, in fact, methyl mercury poisoning.

Already by the start of the 1970s, there was general appreciation of the need to regulate chemical dumping into the ocean and, in 1972, the London Convention on the Prevention of Marine Pollution by Dumping of Wastes and Other Matter was held. Today, eighty-one countries have signed the treaty, which means that the statutes of the treaty are binding for these countries. In 1996, the London Convention was revised and modernized, and amendments to the protocol were adopted. So far, only twenty-eight states have ratified the new protocol but it is expected to eventually replace the treaty from the original London Convention. At the time of the original London Convention, some discussions also took place about fishing quotas, which were aimed at sharing and protecting fish stocks. However, with the exception of these two areas, there was little concern that human activities might potentially impact the ocean and its functions.

This is slightly surprising as, by that time, it was well known that nutrient enrichment from sewage systems and agriculture had a negative effect on enclosed freshwater lake systems in the form of eutrophication (see Chapter 5). However, by and large, there was a consensus among the scientific community that the ocean was large enough to effectively dilute any additional nutrients introduced by man. It was only a decade later, in the 1980s, that there emerged a widespread realization in the scientific community that marine systems, in the same way as freshwater systems, could experience algal blooms, oxygen depletion in bottom waters and changes in biodiversity as a consequence of increased nutrient availability. By this time, understanding had advanced to the point where it was known that human activities could impact bays and entire near-coastal regions and that the effects were not only limited to the ocean areas immediately affected by toxic waste water discharges. In the 1990s, attention turned to the potential ecosystem effects of fishing (i.e. its impact on non-target species and the physical environment, see Chapter 6).

By the turn of the millennium, there was agreement at least in the scientific community that human activities can influence coastal ocean conditions and functions on a large scale and, since 2000, scientists are increasingly aware of the fact that this not only affects the coastal regions, but also the global oceans in general. The increased concentration of CO_2 in the atmosphere causes the oceans to acidify and alters the living conditions of marine animals and plants. This has an impact on biodiversity – which in turn can influence the role played by the oceans in the global element cycles in the Earth System (see Chapter 5). During the course of just forty years, we have gone from the conviction that human activities could not possibly influence the mighty ocean to the scientific understanding that our actions can and do indeed exert a global influence on the oceans.

Hope for the oceans of the future?

The manner in which public awareness of our capacity to do harm to the oceans has evolved does, however, offer some basis for hope for the future of the oceans. Firstly, we have arrived at an understanding of our influence on the biodiversity and functions of the ocean within a comparatively short period of time. Within the space of just two generations, scientists have taken the step from denying the existence of a human influence to establishing an understanding that we exert an adverse effect on this important component of the Earth System. The second important message is that it also only took a relatively short time from when the general population began to become aware of the potential effects of ocean contamination until international regulations were ratified to limit the dumping of toxic waste.

This underlines how important it is for the general public to exert pressure when a legal framework needs to be established in order to control human interventions in the oceans and explains why, in this book, we have chosen to deal first with the lesser known anthropogenic impacts on the ocean and ocean biology before turning to pollution of the ocean with human waste products. The problem of pollution is a recognized problem and there is already a whole range of legislation in place which governs the relationship between humans and the ocean when it comes to pollution. However, in order to develop a sustainable relationship between ourselves and the ocean, our entire society needs to recognize the fact that it is not just pollution, but also a range of other human activities which have an effect on the ocean and its functions. This, of course, does not mean that the dumping of waste products no longer represents a problem in terms of the global status of the oceans.

As explained above, most direct dumping of toxic waste into the ocean is strictly controlled and only possible in a much diluted form. Nonetheless, there is still justified cause for concern about the presence of toxic chemicals in the ocean and the potential threat they pose not only to the marine organisms living in the ocean, but also to the humans who catch and eat these organisms. Despite the legislative framework which limits dumping in the sea, we are still concerned about the possible consequences of, for example, chemicals introduced into the marine environment through human activities. This not so much the result of continued direct dumping of these chemicals but, rather, that there is a growing appreciation of the fact that these chemicals can have biological effects at much lower dosage rates than previously assumed. Furthermore, it is also relevant that many of these chemicals are introduced to the ocean from diffuse sources (from the atmosphere, for example) rather than from point sources. Point sources are relatively easy to control but this is not the case for diffuse sources. Here, we will now take a brief look at the chemicals whose presence in the ocean causes the greatest concern at the beginning of the 21st century.

Mercury

Although the problems associated with mercury contamination have been highly publicized since the Minamata disaster, the potential health risks associated with mercury contamination of fish have again been pushed into the limelight in recent years. It is prohibited to directly discharge mercury into the ocean in most countries. Nevertheless, some quantities of mercury still make their way from the land into the ocean. In addition, atmospheric concentrations of mercury are believed to have increased by a factor of two to three in the last 150 years. Much of this mercury, ultimately, ends up in the ocean in fish – especially in long lived species with fatty flesh. While the concentrations in fish are very low, so that the potential exposure due to eating fish is still very far below the kinds of exposure levels that inhabitants of Minamata experienced, there has been increasing evidence in recent years which shows that even very low exposure to mercury can harm, for example, the fetal nervous system.

Studies of island populations (for example, the Faeroe Islands, where large quantities of fatty whale meat and blubber are consumed) have demonstrated a link between the mercury exposure of mothers and the intelligence (IQ) of their children. The more mercury detected in the mother's body, the less intelligent were her children. On the basis of such studies, a number of agencies, including the Federal Food and Drug Administration in the USA, have advised pregnant women and/or women of childbearing age to restrict their intake of fatty fish.

However, restricting the intake of fatty fish can, itself, lead to another health problem. At the same time that some scientists were discovering that exposure to mercury can be detrimental to developing fetal nervous systems and brains, other scientists were recognizing the fact that some of the fatty acids which can be found particularly in fish with fatty flesh are very important for healthy fetal brain development! Whereas some studies showed a relationship between a mother's mercury exposure and reduced intelligence in children, other studies showed a positive relationship between the consumption of the fatty acids found in fish by pregnant mothers and visual acuity in their offspring.

This presents us with a dilemma: the consumption of fatty fish may, potentially, be detrimental to brain development because of mercury contamination, but not eating fatty fish can potentially have similar detrimental effects because the fatty acids found in fatty fish are essential for precisely this brain development. Further research needs to be carried out in order to gain a better understanding of the value of fish and shellfish in human nutrition and in order to determine the consequences for fetal brain development of consumption/non-consumption of fatty fish during pregnancy.

Mercury is, however, an example of a marine pollutant which has been at the focus of attention for more than half a century and which has seen a dramatic reduction during that timeframe. Nevertheless, the levels of mercury are still a matter of considerable concern, as it is now recognized that what were previously thought to be safe concentrations do actually cause harm. Once again, we see an example of how everything in the Earth System is interconnected – and that we humans are an integral part of it. Who would have imagined fifty years ago that the dumping of mercury in the ocean could potentially be detrimental to the intelligence of unborn children many decades later?

Persistent organic pollutants

Since the drafting of the London Convention, considerably more knowledge has been accumulated about persistent organic pollutants. This is a large group of compounds which remain in the environment for a very long time (as they are difficult to break down), are bioaccumulated (i.e. their concentration increases with every step up the food chain), can be transported over long distances in air or water, and are believed to pose a risk to human health and/or the environment. Some of theses compounds are also believed to be carcinogens or endocrine disrupters (i.e. they mimic natural hormones and/or interfere with natural hormone cycles or hormonally regulated processes). Persistent organic pollutants include insecticides such as DDT, polychlorinated biphenyls (PCBs) and dioxins. This group of chemicals has now become such a focus of interest that a new convention was drawn up on their behalf in 2001, the Stockholm Convention on Persistent Organic Pollutants. This treaty was signed or ratified by fifty states in 2004, who thereby committed themselves to reducing or stopping emissions of persistent organic pollutants in accordance with the targets set in the treaty.

The fact that these compounds are difficult to break down and can build up in the food chain means that the organisms at the top of the food chain (i.e. large carnivorous animals) often have surprisingly high levels of these chemicals in their bodies. The first clear signal that these chemicals were capable of harming animals at the top of the food chain was a decline in the populations of many large carnivorous birds (such as eagles and buzzards but also many seabirds) recorded at many different sites in the middle of the last century. It emerged that this decline was due to reproductive failure of the birds because the shells of their eggs were too thin to allow the embryos to survive. The cause of the thin shells was the high concentrations of DDT in the parent birds. Today, DDT is banned in many countries, and its concentration in the environment has declined significantly in recent decades (although it has not yet disappeared altogether). Consequently, most of the affected bird populations have made a significant recovery.

It is worth remembering this success story in the history of human interactions with the ocean when we consider the future influence of our species on the ocean. A danger for the environment which was caused by our actions was recognized, legislation was passed to remedy the situation, and the bird populations recovered as a result. The most important part of this was, however, the fact that our society responded within an appropriate timeframe. If scientists had not identified the cause of the decline in the bird populations or our society's response had been slower, those bird populations might well have died out. This would have resulted in a regime shift (see Chapter 6), whereby ecosystems with carnivorous birds at the top of the food chain would have changed into ecosystems without these birds.

Two valuable lessons can be learned from the DDT story. Firstly, it is important to understand how a system (be it at the ecosystem, ocean system, or Earth System level) works, i.e. the interactions and connectivities within the system. Understanding these interactions and interconnectivities in the ocean still requires an enormous research effort. Secondly, the DDT example clearly illustrates the potential of human activities to influence systems to such an extent that the system changes to a new state (i.e. a regime shift takes place) and underlines how important it is to manage human interactions with the Earth System or components thereof, and to react before our actions cause such a regime shift.

Today, DDT is no longer a major concern in most ocean waters. However, while DDT concentrations were declining, levels of other persistent organic pollutants (POPs) were on the increase. Essentially, this is a consequence of developments in the field of chemical and plastic industries. In a manner similar to DDT, these chemicals also accumulate in fatty tissue. This means that animals with a high fat or blubber content often have very high levels of these chemicals in their bodies. Just as in the case of DDT and carnivorous birds, there are indications that, in some regions, the reproductive capabilities of some animals decrease at the top of the food chain. Polar bears and marine mammals may have been harmed due to exposure to these persistent organic chemicals (especially PCBs). These chemicals accumulate particularly in fatty fish, especially in semi-enclosed coastal seas such as the Baltic Sea where there is only limited water exchange. Therefore, it is not only mercury but also persistent organic pollutants which are found as contaminants in the fish that end up on our plates.

Dioxins (polychlorinated organic compounds) are another group of persistent organic pollutants which is currently in the public eye. Dioxins enter the environment from many sources, including waste incineration plants, diesel engines, metal smelting, and land sewage sludge which is spread on fields. The smoke resulting from the burning of treated wood and cigarette smoke both contain dioxins. Accordingly, dioxins are ubiquitous, and they are believed to be very harmful to human health, not least because some of them are carcinogenic.

The major source of dioxins for most humans is through food consumption. As dioxins occur practically everywhere, wild animals on both land and in the ocean have relatively high dioxin concentrations in their bodies. There is currently considerable interest in the dioxin content of fish, particularly those caught in enclosed seas like the Baltic Sea. Here, exceptions have been granted which allow the Swedish and Finnish fishers to land fish from the Baltic that have a higher dioxin content than would be allowed in other parts of the EU – but only for use in their own territories.

Similarly, special rules have recently been introduced for salmon from the Baltic, where it is only allowed that the youngest (smallest) fish be landed for consumption. The argument here is that, because of the process of bioaccumulation, the older/larger fish will have higher concentrations of dioxins and other persistent organic pollutants than the smaller fish. Dioxin is also a problem for farmed fish (especially for fatty fish such as salmon) as their feed largely consists of fish meal. As fish meal is produced from wild fish, it contains relatively high concentrations of dioxins, and the dioxins accumulate in the farmed fish. Thus, fish can be a major source of dioxins in the human diet.

Imposex in marine snails

It was mentioned above that some persistent organic pollutants are believed to act as endocrine disrupters, that is to say that they interfere with hormonally regulated processes in animals. There are also some other chemicals in the ocean which have the ability to disrupt hormonally regulated processes. Probably the most important of these is tributyltin (TBT), which for years has been a standard component in the antifouling paints used on ship hulls.

During the preparation of a Ministerial Report on the status of the North Sea in the 1980s, unexpected distributions of some marine snails were recorded and it was discovered that the reproductive systems of many female snails showed malformations. Further analysis revealed that these female snails had essentially developed a penis and that, in extreme cases, the malformation of their reproductive organs was such that the animals had become sterile. This phenomenon is known as "imposex" and is now known to be caused by exposure to TBT. Imposex snails have now been found all around the world's oceans, especially in harbors and along the heaviest shipping channels.

In recognition of the environmental effects of TBT, laws are now in effect in some regions, including Europe, which prohibit the use of TBT on small boats. Larger ships are still allowed to use paints which contain TBT. However, these are currently being phased out and the search is on for a suitable replacement for TBT in underwater antifouling paints.

The TBT story is interesting not only because it again illustrates the unexpected interactions that occur in the ocean system, but also because it highlights a dilemma in the regulation of human interactions with the ocean. Several decades ago, the shipping industry was heavily criticized for dumping large amounts of polluted ballast water into harbor waters. (Unladen cargo ships carry very large quantities of ballast water to ensure that they are stable when sailing without a cargo. As soon as cargo is loaded on board, the water is pumped back into the sea.) After the adoption of legislation which prohibits the dumping of chemical waste into the ocean, this was no longer possible and, today, ballast water is essentially free of toxic materials. This, however, has created a new problem.

Ballast water is now so clean that organisms taken up with the ballast water can survive in the ballast tanks and are viable when they are released with the ballast water into an ecosystem where they were previously unknown. Most of these newly introduced species die when they come into the new ecosystem but, occasionally, a displaced or "alien" species thrives. Often this species has no natural predators in the new ecosystem to which it has been introduced. This means it can become dominant in the new ecosystem, where it may change the structure and/or function of that system.

There are countless examples of alien species being introduced via ships' ballast water with catastrophic consequences. These include the introduction of the zebra mussel to the Great Lakes in the USA and the introduction of a small comb jelly (*Mnemiopsis*) into the Black Sea. The zebra mussel grows on essentially any surface, blocks pipes and adds so much weight to underwater constructions that their structural integrity becomes threatened. The financial costs of combating this species in the Great Lakes is huge. After its introduction, *Mnemiopsis* totally dominated all other species in the Black Sea and brought the fishing industry there to its knees for several years.

These and other examples highlight the risks associated with the potential introduction of alien species via shipping, and the industry is being asked to minimize the risks associated with ballast water. This is not easy, however. Obviously, adding chemicals to the ballast water to kill the organisms present is completely out of the question, as this would mean a release of toxic chemicals to the environment when the ballast water was dumped. Heating is usually not feasible – and would, in any event, increase the use of fuel and, thereby, increase CO_2 emissions at a time when the industry is being called on to reduce emissions. Exchanging ballast water *en route* (so that coastal waters/species are released to the open sea and vice versa) may be a mechanism for reducing the risk of alien species establishing themselves in the new environment, but consequences in terms of increased CO_2 emissions, cost and sometimes safety are associated with exchanging ballast water on the open seas. Reducing the risk of the introduction of alien species with ballast water, therefore, remains an unsolved problem. It is important, however, to consider this in the light of the TBT problem.

We are asking the shipping industry to prevent the introduction of alien species via ballast water but, by restricting the use of effective anti-fouling paints containing TBT, we are increasing the risk of transporting alien species on the bottoms of ship hulls. At the same time, the extra fouling on the bottom of ships which use less effective anti-fouling paints will increase resistance as the ship moves through the water, in turn increasing fuel consumption and CO_2 emissions. The lesson to be learned here is that almost any human interaction with the ocean works on many levels. If we attempt to individually address the various problems discussed here in relation to the interaction between shipping and the ocean, then this will lead to conflicting courses of action. In order for our society to achieve a sustainable relationship with the oceans of the future, we will need to consider *all* of the potential consequences of our interactions. Once all of these interactions are identified, it will be possible to draw up a cost-benefit analysis (including the costs to the environment!) which may help to determine the best course of action for minimizing our net effect on the system. However, we must accept that any interaction of this type with the ocean will always incur environmental consequences.

Not all types of oil are equal

Oil spills are always good for a headline and, therefore, command considerable attention from the general public. This is because many oil types are lighter than water and accumulate at the surface of the ocean. Birds and other animals that live there become covered in a film of oil, suffer, and often die. Images of an oil-covered ocean and dead or dying animals can be sure of a prominent place in the public eye.

Accidents involving oil spills cause quite a stir and a great deal of concern. Interestingly though, accidents also happen at sea which are less well publicized, even though they may also involve large oil spillages. This is because there are certain oil types that, at least in cold water, do not form a layer at the surface of the ocean but, instead, accumulate further down in the water column. Spills of these oil types are not visible either to the casual ocean observer or to the traditional methods used for monitoring oil spills. In fact, one of the only signs of spills of oil of this type is the occurrence of diving birds (and only diving birds) covered in oil.

Nevertheless, thanks to the spills visible at the surface, most people consider oil spills resulting from accidents at sea to be one of the most serious pollution problems for the ocean. In reality however, large oil spills from tankers account for only about 5% of the oil which makes its way into the world's oceans every year. About 10% comes from natural seepages from the ocean floor; the rest comes from human activities. By far the greatest amount comes from drains and runoff from land (i.e. it is transported through rivers to the ocean). Much of this is, of course, associated with our use of cars and the used oil which needs to be disposed of after oil changes. In fact, the annual amount of oil ending in the ocean from an American city of about five million people has been estimated to be about the same as the amount of oil involved in a large oil tanker spill.

Most of the oil transported to the ocean via rivers does not arrive in slicks at the surface. As a result, the consequences are not as plainly obvious as they are when a large tanker breaks open. However, the fact that this type of oil pollution cannot be seen does not mean that it is not there or does not have effects on ocean organisms! Oil pollution in the sea is of concern for a number of reasons, but the most important is probably the fact that oil contains polycyclic aromatic hydrocarbons (PAHs). These are a group of highly toxic compounds which can cause extremely serious health problems (and can even kill in large doses). In addition, some are carcinogenic and some act as endocrine disrupters.

There is, however, some good news concerning this type of pollution. Compared to persistent organic pollutants, PAHs are relatively easily to break down, at least under certain conditions in the ocean. On the one hand, this is done by sunlight, while on the other hand there are also a number of bacteria which special-ize in breaking down PAHs and other constituent ingredients of oil. There seems, therefore, to be a level of resilience in the ocean system to oil pollution. Nevertheless, it should be noted here that oil and its components are not broken down equally well in all waters. Temperature, salinity and oxygen content are all factors that influence the rate at which the oil is broken down. Break-down is particularly slow in cold waters. This means that some parts of the ocean suffer greater damage due to oil than others.

The knowledge that marine systems may have some poten-tial for recovery from oil pollution should not be misused as an excuse for not limiting the anthropogenic introduction of oil to the ocean. Despite this resilience of the ecosystem, there are serious and acute effects of oil pollution on ocean organisms.

It is interesting, given the apparent ability of the ocean to recover over time from oil pollution, that most people imme-diately identify oil spills as one of the most serious threats of human interaction on the workings of the ocean. Undoubtedly this stems from the fact that oil spills are so highly visible. In fact, oil spills from shipping accidents are relatively insignificant in comparison to the quantities of oil entering the sea by other means. In addition, it can be argued that oil pollution is prob-ably not the most threatening form of chemical contamination facing ocean organisms. In contrast to pollution by man-made chemicals such as persistent organic pollutants, oil pollution also occurs naturally via oil seeps from the ocean floor. Organisms have, therefore, over time evolved that are capable of breaking down oil and its components. Consequently, there are natural processes in the ocean which can help the system recover from the introduction of oil. While the mechanisms do not operate quickly, they do exist. For man-made chemical pollutants, such natural degradation mechanisms have not been established.

Therefore, the rather less visible pollution of the ocean with, for example, persistent organic pollutants may, in the long run, be a more threatening form of ocean pollution than the spectacular oil spills we see on television.

Other strains on the ocean

Not all man-made waste in the oceans comes in the form of chemicals. No one knows how much solid debris is thrown into the ocean, but a walk along any beach attests to the fact that the practice is common. A world-wide collection of debris from beaches in 2002 yielded more than 3.7 million kg of litter. From such studies, it is estimated that about 80% of the debris entering the ocean comes from land-based sources and only the remaining 20% from ships and offshore platforms.

One of the problems with litter in the ocean is that marine organisms can become entangled in it. In addition, large animals can ingest debris – sea turtles often appear to consume plastic bags which they, presumably, mistake for jellyfish. A Dutch study found pieces of plastic in 90% of the sampled seabirds – ranging from balloon scraps to lighters and even whole golf balls. In some areas, "ghost fishing" – i.e. when lost fishing equipment continues to catch animals – presents a major threat to marine mammals.

Another problem with litter has only recently been acknowledged: the plastic debris which has been accumulating in the ocean for several decades is breaking down into tiny particles which float in the water or rain down on the sediment. Today, any random sample taken from any sandy beach in the world will be full of it. These particles are eaten by marine life. What is even more worrying is the fact that persistent organic pollutants

(DDT and PCBs) build up on these particles. Measurements have shown that concentrations of persistent organic pollutants on these particles are up to one million times higher than those found in the surrounding waters. The fact that such highly polluted particles are being eaten is clearly a very worrying development, as it allows these pollutants to enter food chains. Ocean litter is, therefore, not simply an eyesore but can also have serious consequences for organisms in the ocean and can, ultimately, contaminate the food we harvest from the ocean.

Noise is another rarely recognized waste product we humans introduce to the ocean. This comes, for example, from ship propellers, seismic exploration of the sea bed, and the use of sound waves (echo sounders) to estimate water depths or locate shoals of fish. The full extent of this "noise pollution" is not known. Likewise, its effect on living organisms has not been quantified. This applies particularly to marine mammals, many of which send out sound waves in order to locate food and communicate with their partners. In some cases, it has been demonstrated that manmade sound in the ocean has the right frequency and volume to drown out communications between marine mammals. Whether or not such the human interaction with the ocean in the form of noise is important in the overall function of the ocean is not yet known. However, this is currently an area of active research.

Summary

While the activities of individuals may not appear to influence the mighty ocean when considered in isolation, the situation is quite different when we take into account the sum total of all human activities – these can and do influence the state of the world's oceans. This is one of the major messages of this book.

We saw in the last chapter that this is true both for fishing and for changes in the element cycles. This chapter has shown that there are also global effects on the ocean resulting from its use as a global waste receptacle and that most of this waste is introduced from land, i.e. into the coastal shelf seas.

The shelf seas are essentially defined as waters covering the continental shelf regions (see Chapter 1). This ocean region covers less than 20% of the Earth's surface, but more than 45% of human population (nearly three billion people) lives along its edges. In addition, 75% of the Earth's "megacities" (i.e. cities with a population of 10 million people or more) are found along the coasts of shelf seas. Coastal waters are, therefore, impacted far more seriously by waste than the remainder of the world's oceans. In addition, coastal oceans are, naturally, enormously productive and it is believed that they account for about 25% of the Earth's global production. As a result, approximately 90% of global fisheries are also located in shelf seas. As we have seen in this chapter, the combination of using the shelf seas both as a waste dump and a source of food for human consumption can lead to an unfortunate chain of events with, ultimately, very serious consequences for ocean functions.

The reason that human activities taking place on a local level can have global consequences for the ocean or the Earth System is simply that the human population has grown to its current immense size. If we take into account that so much human activity is concentrated in coastal regions, it is not difficult to imagine that human activities can and, indeed, do have a global impact on the oceans.

8 Other Human Uses of the Ocean

In the previous chapters, we examined the physical and biological nature of a whole range of processes through which humans make deep and lasting changes to the natural balance of the oceans. We have discussed how climate change heats up the oceans and causes sea ice to disappear and sea levels to rise. We have also shown how the oceans are increasingly being over-fertilized and how they are acidifying. Finally, we have described how the biodiversity in the ocean and the health of maritime ecosystems is becoming increasingly more endangered, and we have discussed pollution of the ocean.

We would now like to take a look at a number of other ways in which humans make direct use of the oceans, including for leisure and holiday activities, as a source of energy, and as a means for transporting cargo. Here, the different forms of inter-action can easily come into conflict with one another or exceed the limits of what the environment can bear. Clever planning, a responsible approach to nature, and integrated coastal zone management can help to avoid these conflicts and problems.

Sun, sand, surf...

Trips and holidays in coastal resorts and at sea are one of the fastest growing areas of the tourist industry. For decades, more and more people have been drawn to beaches, which have hence become a focal point for the development of tourism in many countries. It is not without reason that the "four s's" are the magic formula for tourism: *sun, sand, surf, and sex*. As well as classic beach holidays, many other types of sea-based tourism have developed: sailing, diving holidays, deep-sea fishing, cruises, surfing and windsurfing, whale watching, wellness holidays with thalasso and ayurvedic therapies – the list goes on.

This trend is facilitated by the fact that access to the sea is becoming increasingly easy. Flights are ever cheaper, making beach holidays in the Caribbean, Kenya or Thailand affordable for the masses in industrial nations – and affordability is further boosted by the income gap between the richer industrial nations and these destination countries. In addition, with the aid of modern technology like diving equipment, jet skis, and satellite navigation systems for pleasure boats, it has never been easier to venture out to sea.

Remembering back to Chapter 1, we know that there are already six people for every meter of coastline in the world. If we further take into account that around half of the world's population lives less than 100 kilometers away from the coast, then it is easy to imagine that the growing pressure of crowds of people visiting the coast for leisure or holiday purposes represents a significant strain on many areas. At the same time, it is often precisely a healthy and "natural" marine environment which attracts the numbers of tourists in the first place. Clean water and pure sea air, healthy ecosystems and an abundance of marine life (shellfish and fish, corals and seabirds) are exactly what makes a sea-based holiday such a pleasure. Consequently, the ecological sustainability of tourism has become more and more the focus of interest in recent years.

There are many negative examples of the destructive effects

of excessive tourism. Valuable natural landscapes have been completely spoiled with the unrestrained over-development of cheap resorts. Nesting places of sea turtles have been destroyed in order to make way for hotels. Anchors dropped from tourists' boats destroy coral reefs. Mangrove forests are cut down to make way for golf courses. Scarce freshwater reserves on coral atolls are used for showering, allowing salt water to penetrate into the groundwater. Erosion problems are caused by the clearing of natural vegetation and the subsequent development of buildings. Waste water from hotels over-fertilizes coastal waters, causes algal blooms and destroys coral reefs. Beaches become covered in rubbish. Tourists disturb and scare off timid wild animals. Large ocean liners travel deep into sensitive areas of unspoiled nature in the Arctic and Antarctic, leaving behind pollutants and anchor damage. Last but not least, tourism often also creates significant dislocation and conflicts in the established culture of less developed countries, when the comparatively rich tourists arrive from industrial nations with their own set of values and requirements. The construction of standardized "tourist paradise" resorts spells the end for the established way of life in holiday destinations. Even on the way there, the increase in road and air traffic adds to climate change, with the associated risks of rising sea levels, tropical cyclones, or droughts threatening precisely the holiday destinations at the coast.

Of course, this is a very one-sided picture being painted here. The negative consequences of coastal tourism have already become a cliché, and most of them are by no means unavoidable. Tourism which is carefully managed so that it is environmentally sustainable can even have a positive impact as, in many cases, tourism competes with other forms of land use which are much more harmful. One good example is the sea turtles. Worldwide, these creatures are under threat from poaching and fishing nets but their commercial value as a tourist attraction could help to preserve them. Ecotourism is enjoying growing popularity: watching whales in their natural habitat, swimming with dolphins in the sea, or snorkeling on a coral reef provide just a few examples of the activities this type of tourism involves. More and more coastal regions are moving towards a gentler, more nature-focused form of tourism and have recognized that a healthy marine environment is a fundamental prerequisite if this form of tourism is to thrive economically. As a consequence, tourism management increasingly covers environmental and socio-cultural aspects as well. In view of the increasing commercial importance of tourism and its conflicts of interest with industry, transport, agriculture or nature conservation, use of coastal areas for tourism should be part of a comprehensive and integrated coastal zone management.

Ecologically sustainable planning of tourism development is made more difficult though by the fact that confusingly large numbers of small businesses are involved in the tourism industry. Particularly in developing countries, there is still a lack of planning processes and environmental laws to facilitate coastal zone management. There is also often a lack of the resources required to investigate environmental impacts in the first place, as poorer countries usually have more pressing short-term priorities. This makes the task of a designing and managing the sustainable development of the tourism industry in coastal areas a very difficult challenge.

Cargo transport

In our increasingly globalized world, international work-sharing and the shift of entire production sectors to low-wage countries

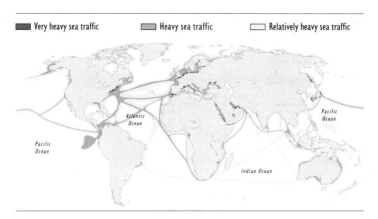

■ Very heavy sea traffic   ▨ Heavy sea traffic   ▢ Relatively heavy sea traffic

Figure 8.1 The world's main shipping routes

have triggered a dramatic increase in the amount of cargo transported across the oceans. The bulk of trade between the large
economic regions of North America, Europe and the Far East is
conducted via the oceans. Around 95% of intercontinental cargo
transport is carried out on ships. The North Sea alone is crossed
by 200,000 ships a year. The amount of cargo transported in
this way is around six billion tons per year, 30% of this cargo
is crude oil. It is expected that trade volumes handled via ships
will increase by a factor of three in the next twenty years. In the
foreseeable future, the Arctic sea ice will, most likely, retreat far
enough to allow regular shipping routes to be set up across the
Arctic Ocean. In April 2006, a German-Russian working group
met on an icebreaker in Murmansk to negotiate the future of
the Northeast Passage. According to calculations performed by
Germanischer Lloyd, this would shorten the sea route between
Rotterdam and Yokohama, for example, by 34%.

Cargo transport places a strain on the marine environment

Figure 8.2 Map of the Northeast Passage with the possible future
shipping route from Europe to the Pacific

in many different ways. There have been spectacular oil tanker
accidents like the *Exxon Valdez*, which ran aground off Alaska
in 1989, or the sinking of the *Prestige* off the Spanish coast in
2002, an accident which triggered one of the worst environmental disasters along the coasts of Europe. The oil tanker
Prestige was built in Japan to a single-hull design and sailed
with a Greek captain for a Liberian owner under the flag of
the Bahamas – making it a symbol for the problems associated with globalization and the necessity to solve these problems with binding rules which apply world-wide. To this end,
there are a number of international treaties and organizations like the MARPOL Convention and the International
Maritime Organization (IMO). As a consensus has to be
achieved between the large numbers of states involved in order
to reach an agreement, the rules set by these organisations
often fall well short of ecological common sense. In addition,

compliance with the agreements reached is often poorly monitored and enforced.

But such spectacular accidents are not even the main problem associated with shipping – even during normal operation, ships release large quantities of pollutants and waste water. A problem which is escalating and has hardly been addressed at all with regulations is the burning of heavy fuel oil to power the ships. This heavy fuel oil is a waste product generated in refineries, which makes it cheap and dirty in equal measure. According to estimates, the sulfur emissions from ships in European waters are as high as the combined emissions from all trucks, automobiles and factories in the whole of Europe. If this trend continues, then around 40% of all air pollution over land will be caused by ships by the year 2010.

While road traffic and power stations are now forced to comply with strict new emissions standards, shipping appears to have been "forgotten" up to now. As it currently stands, ships emit fifty times the sulfur emissions of a truck per transported ton of cargo and kilometer. The oil refineries, which are forced to produce clean fuels for road traffic, simply allow the dirty remainder to be burned in ships – which is why this type of ship propulsion is often cynically referred to as "toxic waste incineration at sea."

As a ship's engines continue to run in order to provide the ship's supply of electricity whenever it is docked in a port, ships now cause tremendous problems in terms of air pollution in many port cities. People who live near ports suffer above-average incidences of cancer, heart disease, asthma, respiratory diseases and shortened life expectancy. Consequently, environmental organizations have been fighting for many years for drastic reductions in emissions from ships, which could be achieved with relative ease by using cleaner fuels and better technology. For the time a ship is docked in port, the best solution would be to provide a land-based power supply so that the ship's engines can be switched off. In the Baltic Sea, an initiative has been set up between eighteen port cities with the support of the EU Commission. Under the name "New Hansa," the aim of this joint initiative is to establish more environmentally sustainable shipping practices and, among other things, to lobby for the introduction of international standards in land-based power supplies.

In addition to emissions of pollutants, the increase in shipping traffic also uses up land area in coastal regions at the expense of valuable salt meadows or mudflats which are so important for protecting birds. Navigation channels are excavated, and the ecology of river estuaries is harmed. In the future, the growing conflicts of interest between port industries, tourism, health care and nature conservation will require that shipping and port development adhere to strict sustainability standards.

Water and salt

Most of the dreams about exploiting different materials from the ocean have, so far, ended in disappointment – from the extraction of gold from seawater in the 1920s to the recovery of manganese nodules from the ocean bed in the 1970s. Of all these ideas, only gravel quarrying in coastal waters has had any commercial significance – that plus the use of the two main ingredients of sea water, water and salt.

Since antiquity, sea salt has been produced with the aid of evaporation basins (salt gardens). This can only be done if the conditions are favorable – which they are, for example, in the South of France, which offers flat coastal zones, plenty of sunshine and little in the way of rainfall. Even today, 20% of table salt used throughout the world is obtained from the ocean.

For us, salt is an essential element of our diet and one upon which we rely for survival. Every human needs between three and six grams of salt per day. In addition, salt can also be used to preserve food and, without it, food can taste bland. As a result, salt used to be an extremely valuable commodity in many regions – this is highlighted by the fact that it was sometimes referred to as "white gold." Entire towns and cities, such as Luneburg in Germany, became rich on the back of the salt trade. The trade routes from salt-rich regions to regions which lacked salt were known as "salt roads" and the Tuareg still cross the Sahara with salt caravans today. The salt trade was an important monopoly right in many places.

The highpoint of the campaign of civil disobedience insti-gated by Mahatma Gandhi as an act of organized opposition by the people of India against British colonial rule was the "Salt March" in 1930, during which Gandhi marched with seventy-eight supporters to the Arabian Sea in a symbolic gesture to make sea salt. The ruling British had secured themselves a monopoly on any form of salt production and trade. During Gandhi's cam-paign, 50,000 Indians were arrested for illegally producing salt by allowing sea water to evaporate in bowls in the sun.

At the same time, humans also need fresh water – not just for drinking water but also in much greater quantities for agricul-ture. As a result of over-exploitation, poor water management and climate change, more and more regions are now suffering from water shortages. For example, a trend towards increasing drought is now occurring in the Mediterranean region; climate models all agree that the greenhouse effect will probably make the problems worse in this part of the world. Water supplies in cities in the Andes (such as Lima) and in the Himalayas are pri-marily based on glacier water. However, the gradual disappear-ance of the glaciers means that this supply will, ultimately, go dry. Would it be possible to solve all water problems by desalinating the inexhaustible water supplies in the oceans?

According to the Bible, Moses performed the first desalination in the Sinai desert: by casting a piece of bitter wood into the undrinkable water from a bitter-tasting source, Moses made the water drinkable. In 1791, Thomas Jefferson published the first scientific description of a desalination technique. However, although it is easy to mix water with salt, separating the two again is much more difficult. The process generally requires a lot of energy and it is, therefore, relatively expensive.

Today, desalination of sea water is used for small-scale applications such as the supply of water on ships and submarines, as well as for large-scale applications such as drinking water purification and for industrial purposes; in Kuwait, it is even used to supply agricultural irrigation systems. It is no coincidence that most desalination is carried out in extremely energy-rich regions where water is scarce, such as countries in the Middle East. Two of the largest desalination plants in the world are the plants in Ashkelon in Israel and Shoaiba in Saudi Arabia. The Spanish government recently gave up plans to build water pipelines from the north to the drought-stricken south, deciding instead to build twenty desalination plants.

There are a number of desalination methods which are based on two fundamental principles: evaporation (distillation) and filtration through membranes. Because the energy requirements are lower, membrane-based techniques like reverse osmosis are becoming increasingly used. Here, the sea water is forced under high pressure through membranes which are impermeable to large molecules like salt. The sea water used to produce drinking water should be as clean as possible, so this increased demand for an ocean service could offer an additional incentive to keep coastal waters clean. Distillation techniques can use waste heat

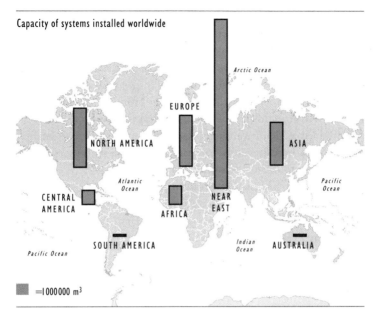

Figure 8.3 The capacity of the sea-water desalination systems installed worldwide

from power stations to operate more cost-effectively. However, of even greater interest for the future are combinations with renewable energies – for example wind energy and solar energy – to ensure that water supplies are not produced at the expense of the climate. Engineers at the University of Edinburgh have recently developed a process which allows the use of wave energy for desalination.

The global capacities for desalination of sea water have been growing rapidly in recent years, and have currently reached a level of around 30 million m³ per day – this is, at least, twice the tap water consumption in Germany. Production costs are falling, with the cost currently around one US dollar per cubic meter. For many private households and industrial applications, this is a perfectly acceptable price. However, it is unlikely that this will be enough to solve the water problems of the bulk of the world's poorer populations, which suffer most from lack of access to clean water. And it is hard to imagine that the relevant quantities required for agricultural purposes could be desalinated – one of the answers here is surely to ensure better water management on the consumption side rather than high-tech solutions on the supply side. In addition, it is important to remember that there is still an environmental price to pay for desalination – in particular in terms of the disposal of the concentrated saltwater residue created in the process, a residue that is often chemically contaminated.

Energy from the ocean

The oceans are already being used to produce energy, mostly through the mining of oil and gas from beneath the seabed. There are 540 oil platforms in the North Sea alone and there are several thousand in the Gulf of Mexico. This concentration of oil platforms is itself not without problems, as they are major sources of oil and chemical pollution to the ocean and the sea bed. Discussions have also arisen about what to do with these platforms when they are no longer needed. In order to fight proposed plans to simply dump the *Brent Spar* in the North Sea in 1995, Greenpeace activists occupied the platform, and there was a widespread boycott of Shell petrol stations, with a loss of turnover of up to 50%. In response to the protests, Shell eventually decided to dispose of the platform on land. Ten years later,

Kurt Döhmel, CEO of Shell Germany, said that Shell had seen a "complete transformation" after this experience, and that the company now followed a policy of sustainable development. In 1998, the fifteen member states of the OSPAR Conference agreed a ban on dumping oil platforms in the North Atlantic. This is an encouraging example which shows how the commitment of environmental pressure groups and the pressure exerted by consumers can make a decisive contribution to preserving healthier oceans.

In addition, there is also the risk of storm damage and oil leaks from oil platforms. In 2005, the hurricanes Katrina and Rita destroyed 114 oil platforms in the Gulf of Mexico and caused major damage to another 69. Thanks to timely warnings, it was possible to stop production and evacuate the platforms before the hurricanes hit. As a result, there were neither loss of life nor major leakages.

There are hopes that the warming climate and the associated shrinkage of the ice cover in the Arctic Ocean (see Chapter 4) will open up easier access to the oil and gas reserves in Alaska and Siberia – possibly the largest reserves in the world outside the states of the Organization of the Petroleum Exporting Countries (OPEC). It would not be without a sense of irony if it turned out that climate change was responsible for opening up the way to even more fossil fuels.

A new source of fuel which is raising hopes in some countries is the deposits of methane hydrates in the ocean bed already discussed in Chapter 4. Although estimates are uncertain, it is thought that the quantities involved could match those of global coal reserves. However, the technical challenges associated with the mining of these resources have yet to be resolved and would involve significant risks. In many areas, methane hydrate in the sediment acts like cement to stabilize the sea bed at the edges of

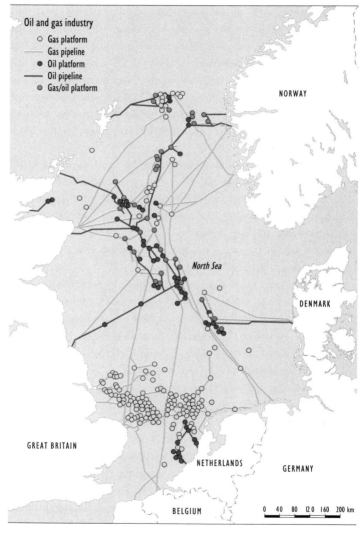

Figure 8.4 The oil and gas infrastructure in the North Sea

continental shelves, so mining could possibly result in underwater landslides. There is also the risk of a blow-out during mining, i.e. an explosive release of gaseous methane from the region underneath the hydrate layer.

The main concern, however, is that methane hydrates are also fossil fuels, so their combustion will lead to further release of CO_2, which, in turn, contributes to the greenhouse effect and global warming. Unintentional release of methane into the atmosphere is also a risk which should not be underestimated, as – molecule for molecule – methane is a twenty-five times more potent greenhouse gas than CO_2 (this is linked to the much lower concentration of methane and the, therefore, still largely unsaturated absorption bands for long-wave radiation). Consequently, the use of methane hydrates does not represent a sustainable contribution towards future energy supplies and, instead, would only worsen the problems described in Chapters 4 and 5. In view of humanity's need to de-carbonize energy supplies, investments in future methane mining would, ultimately, be hugely counter-productive.

However, the oceans can also make a valuable contribution towards CO_2-free and, therefore, more climate-friendly energy supplies. Offshore wind energy has the greatest potential here, and it could be exploited in the near future. Ultimately, wind energy is a converted form of solar energy, as winds are produced by the temperature differentials in the atmosphere which, in turn, are caused by the sun. Of the total solar radiation received on earth, around four percent is converted to kinetic energy in wind form. If we were able to harness just one thousandth of this wind energy, it would cover the global electricity requirements twice over. Almost ninety percent of this wind energy potential is over the open sea.

However, as current wind energy plants so far have to be

anchored in the seabed, this technology is limited to relatively flat coastal waters. If we only look at areas with a water depth of less than 55 meters (by comparison, many oil drilling platforms are now standing in depths of 300 meters), then the wind energy potential of the North Sea alone is three times the current electricity demand of the EU. Of course, there are many different reasons why it would be undesirable and impractical to attempt to cover all our power needs from just one single source, but these calculations show that a significant part of European electricity consumption could be covered in this way. When exploiting different coastal regions in Europe – both onshore and offshore – and feeding the electricity into a powerful grid (the much-discussed European "supergrid"), it would be possible to largely compensate for fluctuations in wind availability across Europe – after all, winds are always blowing somewhere. The existing hydro-electric power stations in Europe would be sufficient to act as a buffer for any remaining fluctuations.

Development of wind power generation on land has been rapid, surpassing even the expectations of optimists. Today, wind farms are technically mature and capable of cost-effective commercial operation in many sites. We have little doubt that this will also apply in the foreseeable future to electricity generated from offshore wind power. If global exploitation of wind power was to continue to increase at an annual rate of 20% in the next twenty-five years (as it has done for the last ten), then wind energy could cover about 40% of global power requirements by the year 2030.

The use of ocean currents to generate power is at a less advanced stage and it also offers a significantly lower potential than wind energy. Nonetheless, it may offer an attractive alternative in some regions of the Earth. Tidal currents are already used in power stations in areas where the tidal range is particularly high. The largest tidal power station currently in use is in the Rance estuary in France, which delivers 240 Megawatts of power and has been in operation since 1966. While these conventional tidal power stations require the construction of a dam and are, therefore, not without their own problems for the environment, tidal power stations have recently been developed that resemble underwater wind turbines and can no longer be seen from the surface. Prototypes have been running for a number of years in Cornwall (the Seaflow Project), Hammerfest (Norway) and in the Strait of Messina between Sicily and the mainland of Italy. The advantage of this type of plant is that it can be installed in many different sites without harm to the environment. Within the space of five to ten years, these ocean current turbines may, possibly, experience a similar exciting development to current offshore wind energy plants.

Projects are also underway to tap into the energy of ocean waves: a wave power station has been in operation on the Scottish island of Islay since 2000. Here again, the technology is in its infancy and the potential is much lower than the potential of wind energy. Nonetheless, this form of energy could become locally important; according to estimates for Scotland, 40% of electricity requirements could be met with wave power stations.

Finally, two more slightly exotic ideas suggest exploiting the large temperature and salinity gradients in the ocean in order to generate power. Ocean thermal energy conversion (OTEC) is the name of a principle according to which the temperature differences between warm surface waters and cold waters from deeper regions of the ocean could be exploited in a cyclic thermodynamic process. In contrast, osmosis power stations would exploit the differences in salinity near to river estuaries, as it is possible to create an osmotic pressure differential here.

One last idea which appears to have more realistic chances for providing energy in the near future is the use of mild ocean temperatures for heating in coastal cities via thermal pumps. During the winter months, some cold regions still record ocean temperatures of around 10 °C, which is similar to the ground temperatures which are used as the basis for conventional heat pumps.

The ocean floor as a CO_2 store

The current climate problems are primarily caused by the accumulation of CO_2 in the atmosphere. Although this gas currently only contributes 60% of the anthropogenic greenhouse effect to date – with the rest accounted for by methane, nitrous oxide and CFCs – it is thought that the CO_2 contribution will steadily increase during the next few decades, as the rise in the other gases is already leveling out. The acidification of the oceans is actually entirely caused by the increase in CO_2 levels. It is, therefore, very important to stop the rise in CO_2 concentration in the atmosphere as quickly as possible.

The main cause of this increase is the emissions generated during the burning of fossil fuels. In this process, CO_2 is not an annoying side effect – it is actually the main product of combustion. The reason that it is possible to gain energy by burning plants and fossil fuels (itself plant material which is millions of years old) is that plants store energy from the sun through a process of photosynthetic carbon reduction. If the carbon is oxidized again, this energy is regained. The oxidized form of carbon is CO_2.

So what could be more obvious than to separate the CO_2 from the combustion gases and lock it away safe from the atmosphere? As well as the expense of such a separation process (that would also swallow up around 15 to 30% of the energy gained during combustion) and transportation issues, the main problem here would be locating suitable storage sites. We are talking about gigantic quantities here; to solve the climate problems through CO_2 storage alone, it would be necessary to capture and store up to 1000 gigatons of carbon by the year 2100 (which corresponds to around 4000 gigatons of CO_2). This is the difference in emissions between a moderate "business as usual" scenario (1500 gigatons of carbon), and a mitigation scenario (500 gigatons). At best, however, only a fraction of this amount could realistically be stored.

For many years, there were discussions about simply dumping CO_2 in the deep ocean. According to one proposal, CO_2 was to be pumped into the Strait of Gibraltar, from where it would sink down to a depth of at least 1000 meters with the salty and heavy outflow from the Mediterranean. However, it is now believed that CO_2 pumped into sea water would not stay separated from the atmosphere for very long, so this would merely delay the problems and pass them on to our grandchildren. In addition, the ecological consequences of dumping would be totally unpredictable (i.e., acidification). As a result, virtually all research in this direction has been stopped; even the USA recently decided to abort their interest in this option.

The situation is, however, different for storage in underground geological formations. Both on land and under the sea bed, CO_2 could be pumped, for example, into former oil or gas deposit sites, which have previously held gas for millions of years. An additional benefit of pumping CO_2 into the ground like this is that it would force out additional reserves of oil or gas (so-called enhanced oil recovery, EOR), which would mean improved exploitation of these sites. Another option could be underground aquifers containing salt water, so-called saline aquifers. Here, the CO_2 would dissolve in the salt water, so it would no longer be gaseous and would, therefore, not force its way to the top. The CO_2-rich water would actually be even heavier than the surrounding water.

But why should we want to store CO_2 under the bottom of the sea, which involves a lot more effort, and not simply on land? One reason is the reduced risk of accidents. CO_2 is life-threatening for humans if its concentration in the air we breathe is 10% or higher. In August 1986, a sudden emission of large quantities of CO_2 occurred at Lake Nyos, a volcanic lake in Cameroon. Prior to this, the water in Lake Nyos had been saturated with CO_2 as a result of volcanic outgassing. Some 1700 people and thousands of animals were killed in the disaster — at distances of up to ten kilometers from the lake. A similar scenario could unfold in the event of a large-scale CO_2 accident on land. In contrast, any accidental release at the sea bed would only cause the released amount of CO_2 to become dissolved in the sea water, which would, at least, not endanger any people.

Opinions are divided about CO_2 storage. Some fear that, by placing our hopes in new technology which is not fully developed yet and will not be available for large-scale use for at least fifteen years, we will put off making the necessary changeover to renewable energies which are already available and, thus, delay a breakthrough in climate protection. In any case, CO_2 storage should not be seen as a panacea, the solution to all of our climate problems, as it can and should only be used within a limited scope and during a transition period. It will only make sense where large sources of emissions (i.e. power stations) are located near to suitable storage sites (because of the high transport costs). In addition, clarification of the risks and sustainability of CO_2 storage is also required. In its report on the oceans in 2006, the German Advisory Council on Global Change (WBGU) recommended that a retention period for the CO_2 of at least 10,000 years would need to be assured (this corresponds to a leakage rate of less than 0.01% per year).

Another important issue here is cost. As was discussed above, wind power can already compete with the cost of electricity generated from fossil fuels. The costs of generating electricity from wind power have halved within a decade and it is believed that they will drop even further as more is learned about the technology, while the costs of fossil fuels are destined to keep rising in the long term. CO_2 capture and storage increases the costs associated with power generated from fossil fuels by a further 30 to 60%. It seems likely that, for economic resaons alone, the renewable energies will represent a more attractive option for avoiding emissions.

Nevertheless, there are conditions under which CO_2 storage actually makes good sense and can be cost-effective, for example in conjunction with EOR technology. In a report from 2005 which caused quite a stir, this is exactly the combination demanded by Norwegian environmental organization Bellona, in order to improve the yield from existing oil fields in the Norwegian Shelf. In return, the report suggested that the proposed new oil field in the Arctic Ocean (Snohvit oil field) would not need to be opened and that, at the same time, this would reduce Norwegian CO_2 emissions. The new coalition government elected in October 2005 largely adopted these plans.

Norway has already been trialing CO_2 capture and storage on a small scale since 1996 underneath the sea bed at the Sleipner platform in the North Sea, 250 kilometers off the Norwegian coast. To date, around eight million tons of CO_2 have been pumped into a saline aquifer there, with plans for a total of 20 million tons. In this case, it makes good economic sense, because CO_2 needs to be separated from the mined natural gas there anyway before the gas can be used and because the Norwegian government would tax these CO_2 emissions into the atmosphere. In addition, the Norwegian company, Statoil, hopes that the additional expertise gained in the process will offer them a technological and, hence, commercial advantage for future CO_2 sequestration and climate protection.

Overall, the storage of CO_2 underneath the sea bed can, therefore, be viewed as the third-best option for climate protection, after improved energy efficiency and renewable sources of energy. In contrast to the other two options, it is still very much at the prototype stage and not yet ready for large-scale use. Once the risks and sustainability have been sufficiently analyzed, it could make an important contribution towards climate protection in a transition period to more sustainable technologies.

9 Visions of the Future

What will the next decades or centuries hold for the world's oceans? It is a famous truism that nothing is harder to predict than the future. There is a lot of uncertainty associated with any predictions of the possible consequences of our actions – even though modern science does allow us to be sure of some things. For example, rising carbon dioxide levels will heat up the climate and make the oceans more acidic. However, the most important reason why the future is not merely uncertain but actually still open is that it will depend on our actions. Fortunately, this book comes with good news: the future is still (largely) in our hands. Consequently, not only can we think about alternative scenarios, we can also choose between different outcomes. We can choose a path to a dark future of rising sea levels and a despoiled, acidic ocean. Alternatively, we can choose a path to sustainable use of the oceans which preserves their vitality and beauty. We would like to close this book by indulging our imagination and presenting a personal picture of two of the many possible scenarios for the future.

A dark vision of the future: the oceans in decline

Imagine a human society unable to learn from its mistakes, unwilling or simply unable to read the signs of unfolding trouble, preferring instead to ignore the warnings of its scientists. Or perhaps just a society that is institutionally incapable of preserving its shared resources and dealing with long-term threats, trapped in the short-termism of its political election cycles and quarterly shareholder reports.

In this type of society, economic development will be driven forward without foresight or precaution. The cheapest fossil fuels will be exploited without regard for the consequences. The concentration of carbon dioxide in the atmosphere will continue to grow rapidly, reaching almost 1000 ppm by the end of this century, partly boosted by positive feedback cycles in the biosphere. This means that carbon dioxide uptake by the oceans and by the land biosphere will decline, leaving a greater proportion of human emissions in the atmosphere than in the 20th century.

Firmly in the grip of global warming, temperatures on the planet get hotter and hotter. At first, the warming continues at about 0.2 °C per decade, as it has done since 1980, but then it starts to accelerate. By the year 2050, global temperatures have crossed the threshold of 2 °C above the pre-industrial value – a critical limit that many scientists in the late 20th century had warned should not be crossed. The warming is very uneven around the globe, exceeding 6 °C in large parts of the Arctic. In summer, the Arctic Ocean is now almost ice-free. The last few hungry polar bears are rummaging through the streets of Arctic towns, searching for food.

Photographs taken from space showing the Earth with a blue North Pole have already appeared on the cover of *Time Magazine* and many other magazines by 2045. The changes taking place on our planet are plain to see even when viewed from millions of kilometers away out in space. Even industry lobby groups have finally accepted that we are in the middle of an unprecedented period of warming, and they also accept that the problem has been caused by humans, but they have managed to convince many politicians that it is too late now to do anything about it. And this time, they have a point. International efforts to curb CO_2 emissions have finally collapsed in the year 2032. The political world has disintegrated into a number of hostile blocks; the great economic powers of China, India, Europe and the USA are all fighting for their own survival, competing fiercely for the increasingly scarce fossil resources. Stricken by devastating drought crises, several fragile states – mostly in Africa – have collapsed, and the more fortunate countries have erected massive border defenses against the rising tide of environmental refugees. A new wave of terrorist attacks on economic centers is fuelled by a widespread sense of despair and unfair victimization in countries affected hardest by the climate crisis.

The oceans show increasing signs of ecological decline. Instances of coral bleaching have become widespread, and many reefs have not recovered. Wild fish from the ocean have become an expensive luxury commodity, only available to the relatively wealthy 20% of humanity.

After rising 20 centimeters in the 20th century, sea levels have risen another 30 centimeters since the year 2000. The Caribbean has become a crisis region, and tourism there has sharply declined due to the loss of beaches and frequent hurricane damage to tourist resorts. Cruise ships are now avoiding the waters affected by tropical storms, but transpolar sea cruises across the Arctic Ocean have become a booming business. China's economic development takes a major setback in 2039 when a category 6 typhoon (a new and stronger category which had to be introduced by the World Meterogical Organization in 2030) destroys much of Shanghai.

By the year 2100, temperatures will have climbed even further, standing at 5 °C above the average global temperatures of the pre-Industrial Age. In high latitudes and many inland areas the temperature rise exceeds even 8 or 10 °C, and the inhabitants of Europe and North America are sweltering in heat waves and troubled by raging forest fires. Unpredictable and strange behavior of the monsoon causes droughts at some times and major flooding at others, resulting in economic disaster and enduring famine in India.

The productivity of many marine ecosystems has collapsed under the double stress of acidification and warming, pushing up the CO_2 concentration in the atmosphere even further. In the North Atlantic, this is exacerbated by a 50% slow-down of the North Atlantic Current and a corresponding decline in deep water formation and carbon dioxide uptake. This type of feedback loop in the carbon cycle now accounts for a large proportion of CO_2 emissions and undermines the desperate efforts undertaken at tremendous cost by mankind to reduce emissions – far too late.

In Greenland and Antarctica, the ice sheets are being depleted at an alarming rate. Ice shelves along the coasts have broken apart one after the other throughout the 21st century, and the rate of water flowing from glaciers and ice streams everywhere has accelerated several times over. Polar bears and many other Arctic species have become extinct. Sea levels are now more than one meter higher than before the climate change caused by humans slowly began in the 19th and 20th centuries. The low-lying parts of New York outside the great storm flood barriers have become a wasteland of ruined buildings occupied by squatters. Kennedy Airport has long been abandoned. Many island nations have been flooded, with their former citizens fighting in vain in international courts for new land.

A bright vision of the future: mankind in harmony with the oceans

Now, imagine human civilization acting wisely and with long-term foresight, dealing with dangers and challenges through good management practices and strategic investments in clean technologies. Imagine that the rapid economic globalization is rapidly followed by an increasingly intensive international collaboration to tackle global problems like climate change, poverty, HIV and extinction of species. Imagine a global civil society emerging which makes sure the shared resources of our beautiful planet, like the oceans, atmosphere and forests, are used in a sustainable way rather than randomly exploited. Is this harder to imagine than the dark vision above? We hope not.

This type of civilization would recognize the planetary crisis it was facing. A crisis just as dangerous to human lives and the future of human society as, say, an attack by aliens. Nonetheless, though, a crisis caused by ourselves, and one that can be mastered if we focus our intellectual, political, economic and technological efforts to this end. Yes, it is indeed a crisis – but the flipside of this crisis presents us with a huge opportunity: the chance to help mankind to achieve a third industrial revolution, and to give it a sound, sustainable and fairer energy system. This would not only stop climate change, rising sea levels and acidification of the oceans, but it would also reduce the international tensions caused by competition for oil and gas, and help to relieve the energy poverty that exists today in many regions of the world.

Imagine that the next few years become a real turning point for climate policy. Finally, heads of state take the issue seriously, not just delegating it to their ministers for the environment. Leading nations draw up ambitious plans and timetables for reducing their greenhouse gas emissions – and they act on them.

This breathes new life into the international negotiations for a follow-up to the Kyoto Protocol. The emerging new economic powers like China and India see that the established industrial nations are serious about doing their homework, and at the same time they understand that they have much to lose themselves if the battle against global warming is lost. So they join the effort.

Thanks to massive Chinese investments in renewable sources of energy, the prices of the associated technology come down rapidly. Within the space of just a few years, developing nations are buying Chinese wind turbines at half the previous price, beating the cost of all fossil or nuclear power generating options. For the next twenty-five years, global wind power generation continues to grow at a rate of 20% per year (as it has done over the past decade), so that by 2030 it covers around 40% of the global demand for electricity. In addition, investments of the magnitude previously ploughed into the search for fossil fuels are now redirected into research into renewable energies, leading to a number of breakthrough advances in techniques for generating energy from the oceans, as well as for utilizing solar power on land. From 2030, solar cells start to cover an initially small, but rapidly growing portion of our electricity requirements, developing a momentum similar to that of wind power four decades earlier.

The renewable energy boom not only provides just electricity, but also new sources of income for many countries in tropical regions. North Africa becomes one of the main electricity suppliers to Europe, generating power along the windy shores of the Atlantic, as well as with thermal solar plants in the desert and feeding it into the trans-European supergrid.

Energy efficiency becomes the focus of innovation in consumer goods. For example, televisions and stereos which consume more than 0.25 W of electricity in standby mode vanish from the market – as outdated "dinosaur" technology which we can no longer afford in the midst of a planetary crisis. Average automobile fuel consumption and emissions finally start to drop again, for the first time in decades. By the year 2030, average fleet emissions of new cars have been halved, and an increasing share of vehicles runs on electricity, a far more efficient technology than the combustion engine. By 2040, almost all new buildings are built to conform to the new zero-energy standard. In most industrial nations, CO_2 emissions are declining rapidly, despite the growing prosperity of their citizens. A turning point has been reached. Carbon prices on the global emissions trading market are dropping, as the technological advances induced by the stringent global climate policies have made low-emission technologies inexpensive.

In 2050, scientists from NASA and the European Climate Center jointly announce that the rise in global temperatures has practically come to a halt, at 1.5 °C warmer than the pre-Industrial Age. The arctic sea ice cover has halved, and scientists are still unsure whether a minimum has already been reached and when a recovery will start. Sea levels are still rising, and all coastal nations are facing major coastal protection costs to raise dikes and build flood barriers, but very little land has had to be abandoned so far. The "Moses" flood barrier system of Venice has to be closed almost half the time, causing some damage to the ecology of the Venetian lagoon but the city is still a thriving tourist destination. At 30 cm above the pre-industrial levels, sea level rise is a serious issue but a manageable one.

In the meantime, important progress has also been made in other arenas as well. Governments have finally recognized the short-sightedness of catching more fish than can be respawned by the fish population, as this invariably leads to a total decline in fish numbers and zero profitability in the fishing industry. Sustainable fishing quotas based on scientific data are now being used routinely in fisheries management, and adhered to with an appropriate margin of safety. In addition, a global network of protected marine areas and marine parks has been established, covering 30% of the oceans. This has given many species zones into which they can retreat in order to recover, and the resilience of marine ecosystems has increased, reducing their vulnerability to climate change and other pressures. In many areas, these policies have led to a gradual recovery of fish stocks and of marine life in general. Pioneering work carried out by Norwegian scientists has also led to great advances in sustainable and clean forms of mariculture, so that the oceans can now provide ample protein for the world's population without fish stocks being depleted.

The decline in the use of fossil fuels and the rising share of renewable energies has had the pleasant side effect for the oceans that the burden of hydrocarbons from petroleum in sea water has dropped, along with that of many other pollutants. Consequently, tourists are able to enjoy increasingly clean waters with more marine life. Some shifts in marine tourism patterns have emerged; in Europe, the noticeable climatic warming combined with the continuing drought and forest fire problems in the south have made the North Sea and Baltic beaches much more popular than those of the Mediterranean. Only few tourists object to the windmills turning on the horizon out at sea; their novelty has long worn off, and most have recognized that the advantages far outweigh the small visual inconvenience.

Final remarks

These are two possible, but conflicting visions. They must not be mistaken for predictions. We are sure that our imagination falls well short of what the real future will bring. However, we believe that it is plausible that the decisions taken by us – mankind – during the next decade will steer us in one direction or the other towards a future which will resemble many aspects of the visions outlined above. Today, these decisions are already being discussed at many political levels – from the global level of the Kyoto Protocol and the Convention on Biological Diversity right down to regional and local levels. These decisions will affect the future of our oceans for a very long time – for thousands of years. Major investments in energy infrastructure are being planned for the next decade, in power stations that will be in operation for decades and will determine whether we travel a low or high emission road until the year 2050. This will determine how warm and acidic the oceans will become, as well as by how much the sea levels will rise. We still have a choice between a reckless experiment with an unprecedented rapid rise in CO_2 concentration and a "slash-and-burn" style exploitation of marine resources on the one hand, and a sustainable future with healthy oceans on the other. The fight over this choice of direction is fought in many arenas – and it is affected by the choices that all of us make every day, when we buy a car or refrigerator, when we plan our holiday, or simply when we talk to our friends about these issues. We hope that this book will help to stimulate these discussions, and that it will help to ensure that the crucial decisions we are all taking affecting the future of the oceans – whether we like it or not – are based on a realistic understanding of how the oceans work and how fragile they are.

Glossary

Acidification: A part (around 30%) of anthropogenic carbon dioxide (CO_2) is taken up by the Earth's oceans, resulting in acidification (decrease in the pH value) of the seawater. This effect can already be measured. Since the start of industrialization, the pH value has already decreased by around 0.11 units.

Aerosols: Substances or particulates which are suspended in the atmosphere. Aerosols are an important factor in terms of the radiation balance in the atmosphere. Aerosols introduced by humans into the atmosphere have a cooling effect and thereby reduce the anthropogenic warming.

Albedo: Reflectivity of surfaces (clouds, land surfaces, ocean surfaces etc.) in relation to incident light from the sun. Lighter surfaces have a high albedo, while dark surfaces have a much lower albedo.

Algal bloom: A high concentration of phytoplankton. Whilst this type of bloom also occurs naturally, it can also be stimulated by human activity, e.g. through the introduction of excessive nutrients (nitrogen, phosphorus). Some forms of algal bloom can cause human illness or can be commercially damaging. This type of algal bloom occurs when the dominant type of phytoplankton is toxic.

Atmosphere: The gaseous envelope surrounding the Earth. The atmosphere of a planet plays a defining role in determining its climate. For example, the surface of Venus is very hot, as its atmosphere is largely made up of carbon dioxide and consequently displays a very strong greenhouse effect.

Bifurcation: In dynamic systems, bifurcation occurs when small and smooth changes to the parameters in the system (e.g. the introduction of freshwater into the Atlantic) cause a sudden change in the long-term behavior of the system (e.g. in the currents).

Biodiversity: The diversity of different life forms (species) in an ecosystem or on Earth as a whole.

Biological pump: The transportation (through sinking) of organic matter from surface water to deeper layers of water or the ocean bed.

Bottom water: A volume of water which extends in the deep sea near the ocean floor, e.g. the Antarctic Bottom Water.

Brevetoxins: Brevetoxins are algal toxins named after the species *Karenia brevis* which is common in the tropics. A dense aggregation of this species can lead to toxic algal blooms and mass fish mortality.

Bycatch: Organisms caught incidentally while fishing for another species.

Calcium carbonate: A chemical compound with the chemical formula $CaCO_3$. Calcium carbonate is very common on earth. It is found in the oceans in mineral form as aragonite and calcite. The skeletons of corals, mussels, and snails are made of calcium carbonate.

Carbon dioxide (CO_2): A trace gas in the atmosphere which absorbs radiation in the infrared region due to its molecular structure, and therefore has an effect on climate even at low concentrations (in contrast to the diatomic primary constituents of the atmosphere, nitrogen and oxygen).

Carbonate pump: The transportation (through sinking) of calcium carbonate from surface water to deeper layers of water or the ocean bed.

Chloroplasts: Spherical inclusions in plant cells which contain chlorophyll and perform photosynthesis.

Climate models: The laws of physics are used to produce a model of Earth which can be used as a basis on which to conduct experiments. The full combination of all physical equations and parameterizations which describe the development of the climate are referred to as a climate model. Due to the complexity of the corresponding mathematical equations, solutions are approximated with the aid of numerical mathematical methods and high-performance computers.

Climate sensitivity: The sensitivity of the climate system to carbon dioxide (or, more generally, to a change in the radiation balance of the Earth) is one of the most important physical parameters of the climate system. Climate sensitivity usually refers to the increase in global mean surface temperature following a permanent doubling of the CO_2 concentration. The most likely value is thought to be 3 °C, with current estimates ranging from a minimum of 2 °C to a maximum of 4.5 °C.

Coastal zone management: The concept of (integrated) coastal zone management describes a management approach focused on sustainability which aims to reduce conflicts in the development of coastal zones, preserve the quality of the environment and support a balance between commercial, social and ecological needs in the development of coastal areas.

Coccolithophores: Microscopically small calcium carbonate algae made up of a single, usually spheroidal, cell, the coccosphere. Among other things, they form a significant part of the chalk cliffs of the German island of Rügen in the Baltic Sea and the chalk cliffs of Dover on the south coast of England.

Convention on Biological Diversity: An international treaty to conserve biological diversity which was adopted at the 1992 Earth Summit in Rio de Janeiro.

Copepods: Small crustaceans, many different species of which are found in the sea and in freshwater. They constitute an important source of food for larger marine organisms.

Coriolis force: One of the effects of the Earth's rotation on motion over extended areas. The fact that wind blows parallel to isobars in regions of high and low pressure results from a force balance between the pressure gradient force and the coriolis force, which is known as geostrophic equilibrium.

Cyanobacteria: A species of bacteria capable of photosynthesis. They are also referred to as "blue-green algae," even though they do not have a cell nucleus and are therefore not technically algae.

Dansgaard-Oeschger events: Rapid climate warming episodes during the last glacial period, named after Willy Dansgaard and Hans Oeschger, who discovered these climate fluctuations in data obtained through ice cores taken from Greenland. During a DO event, the temperature in Greenland increases suddenly by around 10 °C over a period of one or two decades.

Decarbonization of energy supplies: Restructuring of energy systems in order to avoid carbon dioxide emissions, for example through the use of renewable energies.

Deep water: A body of water in the deeper part of the ocean, but still above the bottom water. In the Atlantic for example

the North Atlantic Deep Water is found at a depth of
around two to three thousand meters; even deeper waters are
found for example in the Antarctic Bottom Water.

Diatoms: Microorganisms which form shells made of silicon
dioxide (silicic acid). They form the bulk of phytoplankton
in the oceans.

Dimethyl sulfide (DMS): A sulfur compound which is released
from the oceans into the atmosphere, where it can stimulate
cloud formation and influence the climate. Many species
of phytoplankton produce an early form of DMS, so the
present composition of phytoplankton determines how
much DMS gets into the atmosphere.

El Niño: The most powerful short-term natural fluctuation of
the Earth's climate, El Niño is a large-scale warming in the
equatorial Pacific, which takes place on average every four
years and gives rise to anomalous global climate phenomena.
The El Niño phenomenon is part of a cycle known as the El
Niño/Southern Oscillation (ENSO). The cold phase of the
cycle is referred to as La Niña. ENSO predictions can now
be made, which represents a real breakthrough for seasonal
forecasting.

Emissions scenarios: Sets of assumptions about the future
emissions of greenhouse gases, usually up to the year 2100.
These scenarios are based on current predictions of the
future development of the global economy and energy
systems. Emissions scenarios are not a form of prognosis;
instead, they have the character of different options for
action, as although the emissions up to the year 2100 cannot
be predetermined today, they can however be politically
influenced. A distinction is made between climate protection
scenarios (so-called mitigation scenarios), which are based
on a concerted political effort to reduce emissions, and

business-as-usual scenarios which do not make this effort.
Emission scenarios are used as inputs for climate models,
which are then used to calculate the consequences of various
such scenarios for the climate.

Enhanced oil recovery (EOR): The process of pumping CO_2
into an oil field in order to more completely extract the oil
from this reservoir. In some situations this method can also
be used to store CO_2 for climate protection, which is cost
effective thanks to the dual benefits offered.

Eutrophication: The increased introduction of organic matter
into aquatic ecosystems. As photosynthesis is normally
responsible for the bulk of this, its cause is usually to be
found in an increased availability of nutrients (nitrogen
and phosphorus), as they stimulate phytoplankton
photosynthesis.

FAO: Food and Agriculture Organization of the United
Nations.

Foraminifera: Small, single cell microorganisms, many of
which form shells made of calcium carbonate which end
up as sediment after the death of the organism. In many
areas these shells account for the bulk of all sediment on the
seabed.

Fossil fuels: Fossil fuels are oil, natural gas and coal. They were
formed hundreds of millions of years ago and are burned
today in order to generate power. The combustion of fossil
fuels is the most important anthropogenic source of carbon
dioxide.

Greenhouse effect: Particular atmospheric trace gases
absorb and emit electromagnetic radiation in the thermal
range of the spectrum and thus cause additional warming
of the Earth's surface and the low-lying air layers. The
natural greenhouse effect causes an increase in the Earth's

temperature of around 33° C in comparison to the temperature of the Earth's surface in the absence of the greenhouse effect. Humans increase the concentration of certain climate-relevant trace gases like carbon dioxide and thus increase the greenhouse effect, which must invariably lead to global warming.

Greenhouse gases: The trace gases involved in the greenhouse effect. The most important greenhouse gas for the natural greenhouse effect is water vapor. For the "anthropogenic" greenhouse effect: i.e. the man-made greenhouse effect – carbon dioxide is the dominant contributor with a share of around 60%.

Heinrich events: Sudden events during the last glacial period in which prodigious volumes of ice broke off and slipped into the Atlantic, causing sea levels to rise by several meters. The input of freshwater probably interrupted the formation of deep water – this was shown by sediment data, which also support a cooling in the region of the North Atlantic. Heinrich events were first discovered from layers of small solid rocks observed in deep-sea sediments, which could not have arrived there either due to the effects of ocean currents or wind, but were instead carried by melting icebergs.

Ice sheet: The two large masses of continental ice in Greenland and the Antarctic are referred to as ice sheets. Smaller masses of ice of this type are referred to as ice caps (e.g. in Iceland or Spitzbergen) or glaciers (on mountain slopes). In contrast to sea ice, which is formed through the freezing of seawater, ice sheets are created by snowfall. It is a common misconception to confuse the terms "ice sheet" and "ice shelf."

Ice shelf: Platform of ice which forms when a glacier or ice sheet flows down to a coastline and onto the ocean surface.

This is therefore floating continental ice (see "ice sheet"), not sea ice.

International Maritime Organization (IMO): The international maritime shipping organization is a special organization of the United Nations which is based in London.

IPCC: The Intergovernmental Panel on Climate Change was founded by the United Nations Environment Programme (UNEP) and the World Meteorological Organization (WMO) in 1988. Its purpose is twofold: to document scientific understanding of climate research on the one hand and inform global policies on the other. Many hundreds of the world's leading climate research scientists contribute to the reports of the IPCC. The IPCC reports (the most recent one was published in 2007) are widely regarded as the most reliable scientific reports on the subject of global climate change.

Kyoto Protocol: The Kyoto Protocol was agreed in 1997. It requires industrial nations to reduce their greenhouse gas emissions by an average of 5.2% in relation to the 1990 levels during the period from 2008 to 2012. The Kyoto came into force in February 2005 after ratification by Russia.

La Niña: The cold phase of the El Niño/Southern Oscillation (ENSO) phenomenon. La Niña events take the form of anomalous cooling in the equatorial Pacific and – just like El Niño events – have a global impact on climate.

MARPOL environmental convention: A convention with global reach for the prevention of marine pollution from ships under the patronage of the International Maritime Organisation.

Methane hydrate: A solid form of methane in a molecular cage of water molecules. Methane hydrate has the appearance of dirty snow and can be burned; it is only stable at cold temperatures and under high pressure (i.e. the conditions present at the bottom of the ocean).

Neap tide: The tidal range is at a minimum when the sun and moon are separated by ninety degrees when viewed from earth (i.e. during a half moon). Accordingly, neap tides occur every fourteen days, just like the half moon. See also "spring tide".

North Atlantic Current: A current in the North Atlantic which extends the Gulf Stream (from the western part of the Atlantic) in a northeastern direction toward the coast of Europe. It is often assumed that the North Atlantic Current is part of the Gulf Stream; however, a distinction makes sense because different forces cause these currents: while the Gulf Stream is primarily wind-driven, the cooling of water at high degrees of latitude and the associated differences in density are largely responsible for the North Atlantic Current.

Ocean current power generator: A power plant which uses a type of underwater turbine to generate power from ocean currents. None of this can be seen at the surface of the water. Prototypes are up and running in the UK, Norway and Italy.

Ocean thermal energy conversion (OTEC): A principle for possible power stations of the future, which would exploit the temperature differences between warm surface waters and cold waters from deeper regions of the ocean in a thermodynamic cycle.

Osmotic power plant: A future type of power station designed to exploit the osmotic pressure of large salt concentration gradients in the sea for the purpose of generating power.

Outlet glacier: Large streams of ice through which ice flows
   from the large ice sheets (Greenland, Antarctic) or smaller
   ice caps.

Ozone: Ozone is triatomic oxygen. Most ozone is found in the
   stratosphere (from altitudes of around fifteen kilometers).
   The ozone in these regions absorbs UV radiation which
   would be harmful to humans, and thus minimizes the
   intensity of UV light reaching the Earth's surface. However,
   humans also produce ozone, particularly during the summer
   in the weather conditions typically referred to as smog.
   This ground-level ozone should not be confused with
   stratospheric ozone.

Persistent organic pollutants: A group of chemical compounds
   which are persistent in the environment for a very long time,
   accumulate in living humans and animals, are capable of
   long-range transport via air or water, and represent a health
   hazard.

Phytoplankton: The term plankton is used to describe
   organisms which drift freely in water and are not capable
   of swimming against currents. Phytoplankton is the
   plant variant of this. Phytoplankton is the primary
   producer of the ocean; it utilizes the energy of the sun
   to produce biomass from carbon dioxide and nutrients
   through the process of photosynthesis. Around 95%
   of all photosynthesis in the oceans is accounted for by
   phytoplankton. Its main representatives include diatoms
   (bacillariophyta), green algae, gold algae, dinoflagellat, and
   blue algae (cyanobacteria). See also "zooplankton".

Primary production: The conversion of sunlight and nutrients
   (via photosynthesis) into plant material, which can then
   be utilized by other organisms which are not capable of
   photosynthesis.

Radiation balance: In order to remain in a state of
   equilibrium, over an extended period of time the Earth must
   absorb as much incoming energy from the sun as outgoing
   energy is radiated from Earth. Radiation into space takes the
   form of long-wave thermal radiation. The radiation balance
   is the balance of absorbed and released radiation energy. If
   the radiation balance is changed (e.g. due to an increased
   concentration of CO_2 in the atmosphere, which affects the
   long-wave portion of the radiation), then the global surface
   temperature changes as a consequence.

Regime change: The transition of an ecosystem from one
   status quo to another, e.g. when microscopically small
   plankton replace large, ground-growing plants as the
   dominant photosynthesizing organisms in the water column.

Salinity: The salt content of seawater, normally quoted as
   grams of salt per kilogram of seawater (i.e. in one-tenths of
   a percent, or per mille). In the bulk of the oceans the salinity
   is between 33–38‰.

Salt meadows: A coastal ecosystem on alluvial deposits which,
   despite lying above the high water line, is nonetheless
   frequently flooded. The high salt content in the ground is
   responsible for the unique selection of vegetation, including
   e.g. sea lavender, sea aster, and sea wormwood.

Sediment: Deposited layer of material on the seabed (or
   anywhere else). Deep-sea sediment accumulates over a
   period of many millions of years – in fact, for however
   long it takes until the particular portion of oceanic plate
   is fused back into the Earth's crust under the effects of the
   continental drift. In a period of 1000 years, typically only
   a few millimeters or centimeters of new sediment form. By
   drilling sediment cores it is possible to study the chronology
   of the sediment in detail and draw conclusions about past

marine life, as well as to chart past climate conditions and currents.

Shelf sea: The term 'shelf sea' is used to describe flat coastal seas like the North Sea, which normally have a depth of up to two hundred meters and are positioned over the edges of continental plates.

Spring tide: Particularly high tide encountered every fourteen days when the Sun, Earth, and Moon form a line (around new and full moon). Not to be confused with a storm surge. See also "neap tide".

Stratosphere: The atmosphere of the Earth can be divided into layers according to the vertical temperature profile. The bottom layer up to an altitude of ten to fifteen kilometers is referred to as the troposphere. Just above this is the stratosphere, which extends up to an altitude of around fifty kilometers. The stratosphere contains the ozone layer which is so important for life on Earth.

Subtropical gyres: Enormous, approximately circular currents extending across the width of an ocean basin which are caused by the prevailing wind patterns on Earth (trade winds and the westerly wind belts). At the western edges of the subtropical gyres the current flows polewards as a narrow western boundary current – e.g. the Gulf Stream in the North Atlantic. On the eastern side the current is wider and flows more slowly toward the equator.

Sverdrup (Sv): A popular unit of measure used by oceanographers to measure the strength of currents. One sverdrup corresponds to a flow of one million cubic meters of water per second. By comparison: one sverdrup is approximately ten times the flow rate of the Amazon.

Thermohaline circulation: The thermohaline circulation of the ocean is driven by differences in temperature and salinity of the ocean water, which are in turn caused by surface heating and cooling, evaporation and freshwater input, and by mixing within the ocean. The thermohaline circulation is thus in contrast to the wind-driven currents and the tidal currents. The thermohaline circulation of the Atlantic plays an important role in transporting heat northward and keeping the climate of Europe mild. The North Atlantic Current is part of the thermohaline circulation.

Tidal power station: A power station which uses turbines to exploit the movement of water caused by tidal currents in order to generate electricity.

Tidal range: The difference in sea level between high and low tides.

Trade winds: A wind pattern which blows from the subtropics to the equator. The westerly component of the trade winds dominates more the closer one's position to the equator is. The trade winds in the equatorial band play an important role in the interaction between the oceans and the atmosphere and in the creation of the El Niño and La Niña phenomena.

Tributyltin (TBT): Chemical compound used in numerous so-called antifouling paints for the protection of ships' hulls. Causes sterility and other reproductive defects in some species of snail.

Trophic levels: The levels in the food chain. As the primary producer, phytoplankton forms the first trophic level. Organisms which feed on phytoplankton form the second trophic level, and animals which feed on these second-level creatures accordingly belong to the third trophic level. This concept is important for the marine ecology for a number of reasons; for humans, it is also significant that concentrations of many pollutants increase steadily with higher trophic levels.

Tropical cyclone: A highly organized rotating storm system which occurs in the tropics (although not directly in the equatorial band). For historical reasons tropical cyclones are referred to as hurricanes in North America and typhoons in Asia (see Chapter 4).

Tsunami: A tsunami is a flood wave which is triggered by an earthquake or an underwater landslide (see Chapter 1).

Upwelling: A general term describing an upward motion of seawater, in particular the upward motion of water from deeper layers to the surface. Upwelling occurs in particular along the equator and along coastal regions, and it is controlled by the interaction between winds and the Earth's rotation. Upwelling also plays a very important biological role, as is brings new nutrients to the light-rich (and therefore photosynthesis-capable) surface layers. Consequently, upwelling regions are usually extremely biologically productive.

Wave power farm: A power plant which uses surface marine waves to generate power. One prototype is running in Scotland.

Zooplankton: See also "phytoplankton". Zooplankton is the animal form of plankton. This includes copepods, krill, arrow worms, fish larvae and foraminifera. The record for the largest amount of biomass for a single animal species is held (as far as is known) by the copepod *Calanus finmarchicus*, the lifecycle of which is described in more detail in Chapter 2.

Bibliography

Titles and Internet pages highlighted in bold print are also recommended for further reading.

Archer, D. (2007): *Global Warming: Understanding the Forecast*. Blackwell Publishing, Malden (USA).

Carson, Rachel (1951): *The Sea Around Us*. New York, Oxford University Press.

Charlson, R. J., Lovelock, J. E., Andreae, M. O., and Warren, S. G. (1987): "Oceanic Phytoplankton, Atmospheric Sulphur, Cloud Albedo and Climate". *Nature* 326: 655–661.

Church, J. A., and White, N. J. (2006): "A 20th Century Acceleration in Global Sea-Level Rise." *Geophysical Research Letters* 33: L01602.

Domingues, C. M. et al. (2008): "Improved estimates of upper-ocean warming and multi-decadal sea-level rise." *Nature* 453, doi: 10.1038/nature 07080

Emanuel, K. (2005): "Increasing Destructiveness of Tropical Cyclones Over the Past 30 Years." *Nature* 436: 686–688.

Gill, Adrian E. (1982): *Atmosphere-Ocean Dynamics*. Academic Press, London.

IPCC (2007): *4th Assessment Report (AR4) of the IPCC (Intergovernmental Panel on Climate Change) on climate change (Part 1: Climate Change 2007, the Physical Science Basis)*. WMO, Geneva. http://www.ipcc.ch/

Jackson, J. B. C., et al. (2001): "Historical Overfishing and
the Recent Collapse of Coastal Ecosystems". *Science* 293:
629–636.

Kurlansky, M. (2001) *Cod: A Biography of the Fish that
Changed the World)*. Vintage.

Leier, M. (2007): *Weltatlas der Ozeane (World Atlas of the
Oceans)*. Frederking & Thaler, Munich.

Pauly, D., Christensen, V., Dalsgaard, J., Froese, R., and Torres,
F. (1998): "Fishing Down Marine Food Webs". *Science* 279:
860–863.

Rahmstorf, S., and Ganopolski, A. (1999): "Long-Term Global
Warming Scenarios Computed with an Efficient Coupled
Climate Model." *Climatic Change* 43: 353–367.

Rahmstorf, S., and Schellnhuber, H. J. (2006): *Der
Klimawandel (Climate Change)*. C. H. Beck Verlag,
Munich.

Rodenberg, H.-P. (2004): *See in Not. Die größte
Nahrungsquelle des Planeten: eine Bestandsaufnahme
(Oceans in Trouble. The Largest Source of Food on the
Planet: Taking Stock)*. Marebuchverlag, Hamburg.

Royal Society, The (2005): "**Ocean Acidification Due to
Increasing Atmospheric Carbon Dioxide**". **Policy Document
12/05**. http://www.royalsoc.ac.uk/displaypagedoc.
asp?id=13539

Schellnhuber, H. J., et al. (2006): *Avoiding Dangerous Climate
Change*. Cambridge University Press, Cambridge.

Steffen, W., Sanderson, A., Tyson, P. D., Jäger, J., Matson, P. A.,
Moore III, B., Oldfield, F., Richardson, K., Schellnhuber, H.
J., Turner II, B. L. and Wasson, R. J. (2004): *Global Change
and the Earth System: A Planet Under Pressure*. Springer,
Berlin.

WBGU (2006): *The Future Oceans – Warming Up, Rising High, Turning Sour)*. Special report. German Advisory Council on Global Change, Berlin. http://www.wbgu.de/wbgu_sn2006_en.html

Worm, B., et al. (2006): "Impacts of Biodiversity Loss on Ocean Ecosystem Services". *Science* 314: 787–790.

Picture references

All graphics: Peter Palm, Berlin. Fig. 1.3 acc. to Gill 1982; Fig. 1.4 acc. to Rahmstorf and Ganopolski 1999; Fig. 3.3: © Helge Thomsen; Fig. 4.2 acc. to IPCC 2007; Fig. 4.3 acc. to Church and White 2006; Fig. 4.4 acc. to Archer 2007; Fig. 4.5: © British Antarctic Survey; Fig. 4.7 acc. to Emanuel 2005; Fig. 6.1 acc. to data from the FAO (www.fao.org); Fig. 8.3: © Deutsche Meerwasser-Entsalzung e.V.; Fig. 8.4: © Greenpeace 2004.

In the color section: Plate 1: © National Geographic Maps/NG Stock; Plate 2: © S. Rahmstorf; Plate 3: S. Rahmstorf; Plate 4: http://envisat.esa.int/level3/meris/chl1_2008.html <http://envisat.esa.int/level3/meris/chl1_2008.html> Plate 5: © Norman Nichols; Plate 6: © Michael R. Heath, Aberdeen; Plate 7: © S. Rahmstorf.